William Winter

Wanderers

Poems

William Winter

Wanderers
Poems

ISBN/EAN: 9783337254339

Printed in Europe, USA, Canada, Australia, Japan

Cover: Foto ©Thomas Meinert / pixelio.de

More available books at **www.hansebooks.com**

WANDERERS

THE POEMS OF

WILLIAM WINTER

NEW EDITION

WITH PORTRAIT

NEW YORK
MACMILLAN AND COMPANY
AND LONDON
1892

Typography by J. S. Cushing & Co., Boston, U.S.A.
———
Presswork by Berwick & Smith, Boston, U.S.A.

TO

THE DEAR AND SACRED MEMORY

OF MY BELOVED SON

ARTHUR

———

" My heart, sweet boy, shall be thy sepulchre "

"That's for thoughts"

CONTENTS.

I. LOVE-LAND.

II. Tempest.

III. LOVE AND DEATH.

IV. PANSIES AND ROSEMARY.

V. AT VESPER TIME.

VI. TRIBUTE AND COMMEMORATION.

CONTENTS.

I.

LOVE-LAND.

I.

LOVE-LAND.

MY QUEEN.

He loves not well whose love is bold !
   I would not have thee come too nigh :
The sun's gold would not seem pure gold
   Unless the sun were in the sky :
To take him thence and chain him near
Would make his beauty disappear.

He keeps his state, — keep thou in thine,
   And shine upon me from afar !
So shall I bask in light divine,
   That falls from love's own guiding star ;
So shall thy eminence be high,
And so my passion shall not die.

But all my life shall reach its hands
   Of lofty longing toward thy face,
And be as one who speechless stands
   In rapture at some perfect grace !

My love, my hope, my all shall be
To look to heaven and look to thee !

Thy eyes shall be the heavenly lights,
   Thy voice the gentle summer breeze,—
What time it sways, on moonlit nights,
   The murmuring tops of leafy trees ;
And I shall touch thy beauteous form
In June's red roses, rich and warm.

But thou thyself shall come not down
   From that pure region far above ;
But keep thy throne and wear thy crown,
   Queen of my heart and queen of love !
A monarch in thy realm complete,
And I a monarch — at thy feet !

HOMAGE.

White daisies on the meadow green
   Present thy beauteous form to me :
Peaceful and joyful those are seen,
   And peace and joy encompass thee.
I watch them, where they dance and shine,
And love them — for their charm is thine.

Red roses o'er the woodland brook
   Remember me thy lovely face :
So blushing and so fresh its look,
   So wild and shy its radiant grace !
I kiss them, in their coy retreat,
And think of lips more soft and sweet.

Gold arrows of the merry morn,
   Shot swiftly over orient seas ;
Gold tassels of the bending corn
   That ripple in the August breeze,
Thy wildering smile, thy glorious hair,
And all thy power and state declare.

White, red, and gold — the awful crown
   Of majesty and beauty too!
From what a height those eyes look down
   On him who proudly dares to sue !
Yet, free from self as thou from sin
Is love that loves, nor asks to win.

Let me but love thee in the flower,
   The waving grass, the dancing wave,
The fragrant pomp of garden bower,
   The violet on the nameless grave,
Sweet dreams by night, sweet thoughts by
      day, —
And time shall tire ere love decay !

Let me but love thee in the glow
    When morning on the ocean shines,
Or in the mighty winds that blow,
    Snow-laden, through the mountain
        pines —
In all things fair, or grand, or dread,
And all shall die ere love be dead !

THE LOVER'S CHOICE.

THE stroller in the pensive field
    Doth many a wildering flower descry ;
Sometimes to him the roses yield ;
    Sometimes the lilies feed his eye ;
Sometimes he takes delight in one,
Sometimes in all, sometimes in none.

But when, in dusky woodland ways,
    He sees, beside some dreaming stone,
The fresh, untutored violet raise
    Her pleading eyes, for him alone,
Then makes his heart its final choice,
And nature speaks, in passion's voice.

The lover, when his life is new,
    By many a wayward impulse led,—

Sometimes is charmed by gold and blue,
  Sometimes by brown and mantling red ;
Sometimes proud dame and maiden small
Please just the same, or not at all.

But when, remote from pleasure's whirl,
  He sees, at home's sequestered shrine,
The ardent, happy, guileless girl,
  Of mortal mould but soul divine, —
Too good, too beautiful, to know
How fair her worth and beauty show ;

Then all his roving fancies pause,
  Entranced by that o'erwhelming grace ;
It rules him by celestial laws,
  It lights a splendour in his face :
'Tis the best good that fate can give —
And all for which 'tis life to live !

——•◇•——

QUESTIONS.

BECAUSE love's token is a sigh,
  Doth it the less love's heart disclose ?
Because the rose must fade and die,
  Is it the less the lovely rose ?
Because black night must shroud the day,
Shall the brave sun no more be gay ?

Because chill autumn frights the birds,
   Shall we distrust that spring will come ?
Because sweet words are only words,
   Shall love forevermore be dumb ?
Because our bliss is fleeting bliss,
Shall we who love forbear to kiss ?

Because those eyes of gentle mirth
   Must sometime cease my heart to thrill,
Because the sweetest voice on earth
   Sooner or later must be still,
Because its idol is unsure,
Shall my strong love the less endure ?

Ah, no ! let lovers breathe their sighs,
   And roses bloom, and music sound,
And passion burn on lips and eyes,
   And pleasure's merry world go round :
Let golden sunshine flood the sky,
And let me love or let me die !

NOW.

When you shall walk, in pensive mood,
   The happy paths we used to know,
And sad, regretful thoughts intrude,
   And hopeless dreams of long ago,

How will your wakened spirit bear
Its bitter pang, its bleak despair ?

When in your heart, as now in mine,
  Shall throb the pulse of arid grief —
Since nothing earthly or divine
  In that dark hour can bring relief —
How will you mourn o'er wasted bliss
And that wild moment long for this !

The echo of a silent word,
  An exhalation of the dew,
A lonely sigh at midnight heard
  In depth of some funereal yew —
Those shall be more, in that black day,
Than your true lover past away.

Then do not scorn the present hour,
  Nor crush the roses while they bloom !
The best of time has only power
  To hang a garland on a tomb ;
And all that lasts when years are sped
Is hopeless memory of the dead.

RELICS.

THE violets that you gave are dead —
  They could not bear the loss of you ;

The spirit of the rose has fled —
  It loved you, and its love was true:
Back to your lips that spirit flies,
To bask beneath your radiant eyes.

Only the ashes bide with me,
  The ashes of the ruined flowers —
Types of a rapture not to be ;
  Sad relics of bewildering hours ;
Poor, frail, forlorn, and piteous shows
Of errant passion's wasted woes.

He grandly loves who loves in vain :
  These withered flowers that lesson tea...
They suffered, they did not complain,
  Their life was love too great for speech :
In silent pride their fate they bore ;
They loved, they grieved, they died — no
        more !

Far off the purple banners flare,
  Beneath the golden morning spread :
I know what queen is worshipped there,
  What laurels wreathe her lovely head :
Her name be sacred, in my thought,
And sacred be the grief she brought !

For, since I saw that glorious face,
  And heard the music of that voice,

Much beauty darkens in disgrace
  That used to make my heart rejoice ;
And rose and violet ne'er can be
The same that once they were to me.

DEAD LEAVES.

Not made by worth nor marred by flaw,
  Not won by good nor lost by ill,
Love is its own and only law,
  And lives and dies by its own will.
It was our fate and not our sin
That we should love and love should win.

Not bound by oath, nor stayed by prayer,
  Nor held by thirst of strong desire,
Love lives like fragrance in the air,
  And dies as breaking waves expire.
'Twas death, not falsehood, bade us part —
The death of love that killed my heart.

Not kind, as dreaming poets think,
  Nor merciful, as sages say —
Love heeds not where its victims sink,
  When once its passion ebbs away.
'Twas nature — it was not disdain —
That made thee careless of my pain.

Not thralled by law nor ruled by right,
  Love keeps no audit with the skies :
Its star, that once is quenched in night,
  Has set — and never more will rise.
My soul is lost, by thee forgot,
And there's no heaven where thou art not.

But happy he, though scathed and lone,
  Who sees afar love's fading wings —
Whose seared and blighted heart has
    known
  The splendid agony it brings !
No life that is, no life to be,
Can ever take the past from me !

Red roses bloom for other lives —
  Your withered leaves alone are mine :
Yet, not for all that time survives
  Would I your heavenly gift resign —
Now cold and dead, once warm and true,
The love that lived and died in you.

———◆———

WHITE ROSES.

More strange than death to all regrets,
  Love gives no tear to passion sped :
Its frozen heart at once forgets
  The wronged, the absent, and the dead.

We see the wave that Venus rides —
We do not see the doom it hides.

Fierce, boundless, fetterless, supreme,
   Relentless, glorious, mindless, gay,
Love grants us one supernal dream,
   One vision, one ecstatic day ;
In fate's dull book one fiery page —
Of bliss an hour, of woe an age.

Be the red roses never more
   Companions to a thought of mine !
Behind me fades the lessening shore,
   Above the stars of midnight shine ;
On black and dangerous seas they gleam,
And life is done with doubt and dream.

Pale spectral shapes of dead desire,
   Poor wandering souls of heavenly light,
So lovely in your soft attire,
   So coldly pure, so sadly bright,
Henceforth be angels of my fate,
And take the life ye consecrate !

White roses for the cradled head,
   The bridal veil, the stainless pall !
When love and sin and grief are dead,
   Let the white roses shroud them all !
Ah ! bloom for me while time flows on,
And guard my rest when I am gone.

THE BROKEN HARP.[1]

If this now silent harp could wake,
    How pure, how strong, how true
The tender strain its chords would make
    Of love and grief for you !
But, like my heart, though faithful long,
    By you cast forth to pain,
This hushed and humbled voice of song
    Must never stir again.

Yet haply when your fancy strays
    O'er unregarded things,
And half in dream your gentle gaze
    Falls on its shattered strings,
Some loving impulse may endear
    Your memories of the past,
And if for me you shed one tear
    I think 'twould wake at last:

Wake with a note so glad, so clear,
    So lovely, so complete
That birds on wing would pause to hear
    Its music wild and sweet ;
And you would know — alas ! too late —
    How tender and how true
Is this fond heart, that hugs its fate —
    To die for love and you.

JUBEL.

Surge up in wanton waves to-day,
  Ye memories of a restless past !
In shine and shadow glance and play, —
  This golden moment is your last.

Float, phantoms, o'er a sapphire sea, —
  Remembered joy, remembered pain,
Passions and fears that used to be,
  But never can be mine again !

Sweet visions, faded long ago,
  So beautiful, and once so dear, —
That wrought alike my bliss and woe, —
  Your welcome and farewell are here.

For now no more can fancy wile
  My steadfast heart with dreams untrue :
I give you each a parting smile,
  I give you all a glad adieu.

As one whose soul, on vibrant wings
  Of new-born freedom, mounts the skies,
Spurning the earth, my spirit springs
  To scale the peaks of paradise.

The sunshine wraps me in its arms,
  Wild winds of power around me blow,

And heaven's ablaze with starry charms
  To bless the path whereon I go.

For mine is now the ardent truth
  And secret of the lover's kiss ;
The valley of immortal youth ;
  The sacred mountain-height of bliss !

VICTORIA.

MIDNIGHT and moonlight encircle her slum-
    bers,
  Pillowed, afar, on the wandering deep :
Softly, ah softly, with tenderest numbers,
  Echoes of paradise, lull her to sleep !

Stars in your lustre and clouds in your
    fleetness,
  Mix round the gallant ship, breasting the
    gale !
Shed your sweet influence over her sweet-
    ness !
  Guard every pinion and bless every sail !

Billows, roll gently, that bear on your
    bosom
  Treasure more precious than infinite
    gold —

Beauty in spring-time and love in its blos-
  som,
  All that my hungry heart longs to enfold.

Ocean, that breaks on the rocks where I
  languish,
  Blessing and prayer on your surges to
  pour,
Like, in your might, to my passionate anguish,
  Shield her, and save her, and waft her to
  shore !

Angels, that float in the heavenly spaces,
  Ah, while you guide her through perils
  unknown,
Still let the light of your beautiful faces
  Shine on her face that is fair as your
  own !

Violets, welcome her ! roses, adore her —
  Blushing with rapture from mountain to
  sea !
Lilies, flash out on the meadows before her,
  Sparkle in glory, and ripple in glee !

Proudly she comes, like the pageant of
  morning
  Borne through the pearl-purpled gates of
  the day !

Darkness and sorrow, consumed in her
    scorning,
  Shrink from her splendour and vanish
    away.

Scattered o'er mountain and forest and
    river,
  Far the dark phantoms of trouble are
    hurled :
She will illuminate, she will deliver,
  She will redeem and transfigure the
    world !

AN ANGEL BRIDE.

HER young face is softly fair —
  Pearl of morning flushed with red —
And the brown and silken hair
  Hovers mist-like round her head.

Crimson lips, like rubies bright,
  Smiling, part o'er tiny pearls ;
Little wandering stars of light
  Love to nestle in her curls.

And her voice is soft and low,
  Clear as music and as sweet ;

Hearing it, you hardly know
   Where the sound and silence meet

All the magic who can tell
   Of her laughter and her sighs,
Or what heavenly meanings dwell
   In her kind, confiding eyes!

All her ways are winning ways,
   Full of tenderness and grace;
And a witching sweetness plays
   Fondly o'er her gentle face.

True and pure her soul within, —
   Breathing a celestial air!
Evil and the shame of sin
   Could not dwell a moment there.

Is it but a vision, this?
   Fond creation of the brain?
Phantom of a fancied bliss?
   Type of beauty void and vain?

No! the tides of being roll
   Toward a paradise to be,
Where this idol of my soul
   Waits and longs for love and me.

C

A WISH.

THINK of me as your friend, I pray,
  And call me by a tender name:
I will not care what others say,
  If only you remain the same !
I will not care how dark the night,
  I will not care how wild the storm:
Your love will fill my heart with light,
  And shield me close, and keep me warm.

Think of me as your friend, I pray,
  For else my life is little worth:
So shall your memory light my way,
  Although we meet no more on earth:
For while I know your faith secure,
  I ask no happier fate to see:
Thus to be loved by one so pure
  Is honour rich enough for me.

VIOLET.

ONE name I shall not forget —
Gentle name of Violet.

Many and strange the years have sped:
She who bore that name is dead:

Dead — and resting by the sea,
Where she gave her heart to me:

Dead — and now the grasses wave,
And the dry leaves, o'er her grave,

Rustling in the autumn wind,
Like the sad thoughts in my mind.

She was light and soon forgot;
Loved me well and loved me not:

Changeful as the April sky —
Kind or cruel, sad or shy;

Gray-eyed, winsome, arch, and fair —
My youth's passion and despair.

Now, through storms of many years,
Now, through tender mist of tears,

Looking backward, I can see
She was always true to me.

Yet, with prisoned tears that burn,
Cold we parted, wayward, stern;

Spoke the fatal farewell word,
Neither meant and neither heard;

Spoke — and parted in our pain,
Nevermore to meet again.

Sometimes, underneath the moon,
On rose-laden nights of June, —

When white clouds drift o'er the blue,
While the pale stars glimmer through,

And the honeysuckle throws
Fragrant challenge to the rose,

And the liberal pine-tree flings
Perfume on the midnight's wings, —

Came, with thrills of hope and fear,
Mystic sense that she was near;

Came the thought, — 'Through good and ill
She loves, and she remembers still!'

But no word e'er came or went;
And, when nine long years were spent,

Something in my bosom said,
Very softly, 'she is dead!'

Now, at sombre autumn eve,
Wandering where the woodlands grieve,

Or where wild winds whistle free,
On the hills that front the sea,

Cruel thoughts of love and loss
Nail my spirit to the cross.

Friends have fallen, youth is gone,
Fields are brown and skies are wan:

One name I shall not forget —
Gentle name of Violet.

CHANGED.

I.

It is not that she's far away
That breaks my heart and dims my day;
It is that there is something gone
Her passion used to dream upon;
That now the tender dream is o'er,
And him she loved she loves no more.

II.

Her absence makes my spirit mourn —
Yet e'en her absence could be borne:
But, — bleakest of all human grief,
And desolate beyond relief, —
One thought consumes my bosom's core —
That him she loved she loves no more.

III.

The violets should be bluer far,
The roses redder than they are,
And lighter o'er the rippling grass
The shadows of the clouds should pass.
There's nothing as it was before —
For him she loved she loves no more.

LOVE'S REFUGE.

I.

SET your face to the sea, fond lover, —
  Cold in darkness the sea-winds blow !
Waves and clouds and the night will cover
  All your passion and all your woe:
Sobbing waves and the death within them,
  Sweet as the lips that once you prest—
Pray that your hopeless heart may win
    them !
  Pray that your weary life may rest !

II.

Set your face to the stars, fond lover, —
  Calm, and silent, and bright, and true ! —
They will pity you, they will hover
  Softly over the deep for you.
Winds of heaven will sigh your dirges,
  Tears of heaven for you be spent ;
Sweet, for you, will the murm'ring surges
  Pour the wail of their low lament.

LOVE'S REQUIEM.

I.

BRING withered autumn leaves,
Call everything that grieves,

And build a funeral pyre above his head !
  Heap there all golden promise that de-
    ceives,
  Beauty, that wins the heart and then be-
    reaves, —
      For Love is dead.

II.

Not slowly did he die :
A meteor from the sky
Falls not so swiftly as his spirit fled,
  When, with regretful, half-averted eye,
  He gave one little smile, one little sigh,
    And so was sped.

III.

But oh, not yet, not yet
Would my lost soul forget
How beautiful he was while he did live ;
  Or, when his eyes were dewy and lips wet,
  What kisses, tenderer than all regret,
    My love would give.

IV.

Strew roses on his breast !
He loved the roses best ;

He never cared for lilies or for snow.
 Let be this bitter end of his sweet quest;
 Let be the pallid silence that is rest —
  And let all go !

———◦◦◦———

THE UNDERTONE.

It droops and dies in morning light —
 The rose that yesterday was whole :
'Ah, whither, on the wind of night,
 Is borne the fragrance of my soul ?'

It sinks upon the ocean zone —
 The wind that marred the tender rose :
' Ah, whither has the fragrance flown,
 And what shall give my soul repose ?'

It breaks upon the rocky shore —
 The vast, tumultuous, grieving sea :
'Ah, never, never, never more
 Can love and peace come back to me !'

It sobs, far up the lonely sky,
 It faints in regions of the blest —
The endless, bitter, human cry,
 —And only Death could tell the rest.

CONSTANCE.

WITH diamond dew the grass was wet, —
  'Twas in the spring and gentlest
      weather, —
And all the birds of morning met,
  And carolled in her heart together.

The wind blew softly o'er the land,
  And softly kissed the joyous ocean :
He walked beside her on the sand,
  And gave and won a heart's devotion.

The thistledown was in the breeze,
  With birds of passage homeward flying :
His fortune lured him o'er the seas,
  And on the shore he left her, sighing.

She saw his barque glide down the bay,
  Through tears and fears she could not
      banish ;
She saw his white sails melt away —
  She saw them fade, she saw them vanish.

And ' Go,' she said, ' for winds are fair,
  And love and blessing round you hover ;
When you sail backward through the air,
  Then I will trust the word of lover.'

Still ebbed, still flowed, the tide of years,
   Now chilled with snows, now bright with
      roses,
And many smiles were turned to tears,
   And sombre morns had radiant closes.

And many ships came sailing by,
   With many a golden promise freighted ;
But nevermore from sea or sky
   Came love, to bless her heart that waited.

Yet on, by tender patience led,
   Her sacred footsteps walked, unbidden,
Wherever sorrow bows its head,
   Or want, and care, and shame are hidden.

And they who saw her snow-white hair,
   And dark, sad eyes, so deep with feeling,
Breathed all at once the chancel air
   And seemed to hear the organ pealing.

Till once, at shut of autumn day,
   In marble chill she paused and hearkened,
With startled gaze where far away
   The wastes of sky and ocean darkened.

There, for a moment, faint and wan,
   High up in air and landward striving,

Stern-fore a spectral barque came on,
   Across the purple sunset driving.

Then something out of night she knew,
   Some whisper heard, from heaven de-
      scended,
And peacefully as falls the dew
   Her long and lonely vigil ended.

The violet and the bramble-rose
   Make glad the grass that dreams above
      her ;
And, freed from time and all its woes,
   She trusts again the word of lover.

AFTER ALL.

THE apples are ripe in the orchard,
   The work of the reaper is done,
And the golden woodlands redden
   In the blood of the dying sun.

At the cottage door the grandsire
   Sits, pale, in his easy-chair,
While a gentle wind of twilight
   Plays with his silver hair.

A woman is kneeling beside him ;
  A fair young head is prest,
In the first wild passion of sorrow,
  Against his agéd breast.

And far from over the distance
  The faltering echoes come,
Of the flying blast of trumpet
  And the rattling roll of drum.

Then the grandsire speaks, in a whisper, —
  'The end no man can see ;
But we give him to his country,
  And we give our prayers to Thee.' . . .

The violets star the meadows,
  The rose-buds fringe the door,
And over the grassy orchard
  The pink-white blossoms pour.

But the grandsire's chair is empty,
  The cottage is dark and still,
There's a nameless grave in the battle-field,
  And a new one under the hill.

And a pallid, tearless woman
  By the cold hearth sits, alone ;
And the old clock in the corner
  Ticks on with a steady drone.

NO MORE.

I.

THEY walked beside the summer sea
  And watched the slowly dying sun ;
And ' O,' she said, ' come back to me,
  My love, my own, my only one ! '
But, while he kissed her fears away,
  The gentle waters kissed the shore,
And, sadly whispering, seemed to say,
    He'll come no more! he'll come no
    more !

II.

Alone beside the autumn sea
  She watched the sombre death of day ;
And ' O,' she said, ' remember me,
  And love me, darling, far away ! '
A cold wind swept the wat'ry gloom,
  And, darkly whispering on the shore,
Sighed out the secret of his doom, —
    He'll come no more! he'll come no
    more !

III.

In peace beside the winter sea
  A white grave glimmers to the moon ;
And waves are fresh, and clouds are free,
  And shrill winds pipe a careless tune.

One sleeps beneath the dark blue wave,
   And one upon the lonely shore;
But, joined in love, beyond the grave,
   They part no more! they part no more!

THE LAST SCENE.

HERE she slumbers, white and chill;
   Put your hand upon her brow;
Her sad heart is very still,
   And she does not know you now.

Ah, the grave's a quiet bed;
   She will sleep a pleasant sleep,
And the tears that you may shed
   Will not wake her, — therefore weep!

Weep, — for you have wrought her woe;
   Mourn, — she mourned and died for you:
Ah, too late we come to know
   What is false and what is true!

RUE.

THE autumn wind is moaning in the leaves,
   And the long grass is rustling on my
      grave:

Ah, would you have me think your heart
    now grieves
  For her your waning passion would not
    save ?

For I am dead ; know you not I am dead ?
  Why will you haunt me in my rest to-
    night, —
Standing above, and listening overhead,
  Where I am buried deep and out of
    sight ?

Have you not wine and music, in your
    home,
  And her fair form, and eyes so pure and
    proud
With love of you ? and wherefore do you
    roam
  To vex me, lying silent in my shroud ?

Seek your new love ! She calls you, and
    the tears
  Are warm on her pale face, and her young
    breast
Is full of doubt and sorrow — for she
    hears
  Low-whispered words, that startle her
    from rest.

In from the night ! the storm begins to stir :
　I will be near, and ghostly eyes shall see
How you will kiss her lips, and say to her,
　' Thine always, love,' as once you said to
　　me.

ASLEEP.

I.

HE knelt beside her pillow, in the dead
　watch of the night,
And he heard her gentle breathing, but her
　face was still and white,
And on her poor, wan cheek a tear told
　how the heart can weep,
And he said, ' My love was weary — God
　bless her ! she's asleep.'

II.

He knelt beside her grave-stone, in the
　shuddering autumn night,
And he heard the dry grass rustle, and his
　face was thin and white,
And through his heart the tremor ran of
　grief that cannot weep,
And he said, ' My love was weary — God
　bless her ! she's asleep.'

EBB TIDE.

In dusky gloom she sits apart,
   Beyond the moonlight's silver glow ;
And tender fancies break her heart,
   That bloomed, and withered, long ago.

Her patient eyes are wet with tears,
   Her face is pale with want and care,
And all the griefs of all her years,
   Transfigured, crown her snowy hair.

Gaunt sorrow claims her, heart and brain ;
   She bears the burden of the cross ;
She hears a solemn dirge of pain,
   The sad, old song of love and loss.

So glide the lonesome hours away :
   The song is still, the grief is past ;
Alike to her are night and day —
   And life and trouble rest at last.

D

II.

TEMPEST.

II.

TEMPEST.

DOOM.

A RAVEN flew over the house-top,
　In the gloaming that heralds the night:
Far off snarled the threat of the thunder,
　And the raven he croaked in his flight.

A raven flew over the house-top,
　And his shadow fell dark on my heart:
A voice, in its innermost chamber,
　Said, ' The angel of love must depart.'

Too long you are calm in the sunshine,
　And too long are the roses in bloom:
Time now for the rush of the tempest,
　For the chill, and the blight, and the
　　gloom.' . . .

Deserted the house is and silent;
　Night is drifting o'er woodland and wave:
And love, that was life's consecration,
　Is a spectre that broods on a grave.

53

CIRCE.

It is the law of streams to run,
    Of autumn leaves to fall;
And she who has been false to one —
    She will be false to all.

O, wild as tempest on the sea
    Is that poor lover's fate,
Whose faithful spirit, bound to thee,
    Must hope, and fear, and wait!

By surge of joy and storm of pain
    His heart is soothed or broke;
He would not rend thy heavenly chain —
    He cannot bear thy yoke.

There is no heaven so high as faith,
    No hell so deep as doubt,
No haunted spectre like the wraith
    Thy fancies wile or flout!

Ah, let that tiger heart of thine,
    By brutish mercy led,
To just one piteous act incline —
    And strike thy lover dead!

Then, let the streams forever run,
  The leaves forever fall !
Thou wilt — at last — be true to one,
  And not be false to all.

———◆◆◆———

SEMPER IDEM.

I.

THIS is the place where he brought her
    home,
  Home, — but not to his heart, I know :
For it cannot be but her memories roam
  To the first and the true love, long ago !
Noble and lovely and wretched bride,
  Doomed, in her gorgeous palace of stone,
Loveless forever, to sit by his side,
  And yet be, forever and ever, alone !

II.

Noble and beautiful spirit of love !
  Well, I can wish you were happy, —
    though
I stand out here, while the stars above
  Are as white and cold as the ground
    below.

I am glad that the splendour is all your
    own;
    I do not desire it — ah, not I !
But am well content, at the foot of your
    throne,
    To sink in the frozen street and die.

III.

Perhaps you would see me, then — who
    knows ?
    Perhaps you would see, in my haggard
    face,
Whence they have risen — your subtle
    woes,
    And the something that saddens your
    stately grace.
Perhaps — ah me, I am bold indeed ! —
    Perhaps you would touch me ! Heart
    and brain !
I am sure it would make the old wound
    bleed,
    If it did not wake me to life again !

IV.

Lost — but I love you, all the same:
    'Twas a faithful heart that you threw
    away :

I can say it now, and with nothing of shame,
  For I shall not live to another day.
I can say, though the night of grief was long,
  That the light of morning struggles
    through ;
And, lifted out of my sorrow and wrong,
  If I cannot live, I can die, for you !

——•◦•——

ACROSS THE PALL.

Now she lies here, dead before you,
  Motionless and gray as stone ;
Now the cruel grief broods o'er you,
  Stricken, agonised, and lone ;
Now that passion's dream is past,
Well it is we meet at last !

Ay, you loved her — loved her truly —
  With the utmost faith of man ;
Sacrificing all things, duly,
  As a noble lover can !
And she made you — what I see ;
What 'tis well that you can be.

Loved her ! Virtue, truth, and honour,
  Sense, and manhood — what are they ?

Stand up here and look upon her!
  'Tis a pretty piece of clay.
Others, quite as fond and true,
Loved her, quite as well as you.

So I pity you, poor dreamer
  (Dreams, the longest, are not long),
And I would not make it seem her
  Guilt, that e'er she did me wrong.
She was heavenly — cloud and star —
She was what the angels are.

Hope and wait; and when you meet her,
  With them, in the Eden plain,
Clasp her to your soul, and greet her
  With a word of noble pain.
Tell her, in yon starry cope,
That I taught you how to hope.

Time and tide flow on forever;
  Pleasure's ghost is always pain;
Life is fevered with endeavour,
  Sad with loss and sweet with gain.
But there is no certain bliss
In this world for only this.

Look up bravely where, forgiven,
  Erring hearts repentant rest:

Only love and trust find heaven !
  Still the faithful are the blest :
Faithful love, that ransoms you,
Well may save your idol too.

But, for me there is no morrow,
  Crown of love nor crown of fame :
I must tread a mighty sorrow
  In the mire of sensual shame.
Down I grovel on the earth,
Wasting toward a brutish birth.

'Tis a world of commonplaces,
  Empty hearts, and shallow brains,
Flaunting fools with specious faces,
  Black desires and crimson stains :
When I found that heart untrue,
Love itself was falsehood too.

Always round us are the curses,
  And the long, tumultuous roar :
We are jostled in our hearses,
  Even as we were before.
They alone escape the strife
Who attain the spirit's life.

Hope, I say, till you receive her ;
  Hope, — for we are only men.

Lay her in the grave, and leave her
  Just your heart, to keep till then.
Take my blessing — for I know
All your love and all your woe.

————◦◦◦————

THE YELLOW ROSE.

I.

Ah, had we met in other days, before my
    soul had known
What 'tis to smile o'er ruined hopes, in
    mockery and alone,
Perchance it then had been my lot, which
    now can never be,
To make thy heart, that beats for none,
    beat warm and true for me.

II.

But now the shadows round my way are
    gathering dark and grim,
The wind blows coldly off the shore, the
    lights are growing dim,
The angry waters rage and roar, and head-
    long through the night
From love, from hope, from thee, my
    barque goes plunging out of sight.

III.

And so I waft my fond farewell across the
    darkening brine :
Thy heart can never, never bring the peace
    of love to mine :
There is no peace for evermore, in earth or
    heaven, for me —
But, oh, if this could once have been, how
    lovely life would be !

IV.

I see thee on the distant shore, in all thy
    glittering grace,
The sunshine streaming round thy form,
    and hope upon thy face ;
And I shall see those glorious eyes and hear
    that voice divine
Till fate has stilled this wayward heart, —
    but true till death to thine.

V.

Nor chance nor change can ever dim the
    glory of that brow ;
The light will shine forever there that
    shines upon thee now ;
And tempest-tossed and far away upon the
    sea of sin
I yet shall know, though lost to me, there
    was a heaven to win.

VI.

I did not think that time or grief could
    ever break the pride
That lets my soul reveal the truth it now
    no more can hide,
But lonely o'er the wreck of youth its fires
    are burning yet —
And, well for me if I had died or ever we
    had met !

THE WRECKER'S BELL.

I.

There's a lurid light in the clouds to-night,
    In the wind there's a desolate moan ;
And the rage of the furious sea is white,
    Where it beats on the crags of stone :
Stand here at my side, and look over the
    tide,
    And say if you hear it, — the sullen knell,
Faint, from afar, on the harbour-bar,
    The hollow boom of the wrecker's bell.
For I cannot hear — I am cold with fear —
    Ah, leave me not alone !
For I'm old, I'm old, and my blood is cold,
    And I fear to be alone.

II.

With a shudder I saw his ashen face,
  In that wild and fearful night —
For his blazing eyes illumed the place
  With a terrible, ghastly light;
And ever his long locks floated out,
  As white as the foam of the sea ;
And the great waves dashed on the rocks
    about
  With a mad and cruel glee.
But I stood by his side, and looked over
    the tide,
  And faintly I heard that solemn knell,
Faint, from afar, on the harbour-bar,
  The hollow boom of the wrecker's bell.

III.

It is but the clang of the signal bell,
  That floats through the midnight air:
For many a year in the surging swell
  Has the old bell sounded there.
When the storm in his might rides through
    the night
  And his steeds in thunder neigh,
Then its iron tongue is swayed and swung,
  And plunged in the angry spray ;
And so when the summer skies are bright,
  And the breakers are at play.

But wherefore is it you stay me here,
   And why do you shudder and moan,
And what are the nameless shapes you
     fear
   In this desolate place alone ?
For your eyes are set in a dreadful glare,
   And you shrink at the solemn knell,
As it trembles along the midnight air —
   The boom of the wrecker's bell.

IV.

Look up, he cried, to the awful sky,
   Look over the furious sea,
And mark, as the grinning fiends float
     by,
   How they beckon and howl to me !
They are ringing my knell with the baleful
     bell,
   And they gloat on the doom to be.
Ah ! give me your hand, and look not
     back —
   We stand not here alone —
And the horrible shapes that throng my
     track
   Would turn your heart to stone.
The spell of the dead is on the hour,
And I yield my soul to its fearful power.

V.

A face looks forth in the darkness there,
    A young face, sweet with a rosy light:
The sunshine sleeps in her golden hair,
    And her violet eyes are softly bright:
On her parted lips there's an innocent smile,
    Like a sunbeam kissing a velvet rose ;
And her cheeks of pearl grow warm the
        while,
    With a delicate blush that comes and
        goes.
Ah ! purer than morn in its purest hour,
    And holy as one from an angel clime,
Was the tender woman, the beautiful
        flower,
    I loved and lost in the far-off time.

VI.

One fatal night, in the long ago,
    My gallant cruiser passed that bar.
In a bank of clouds the moon hung low,
    And the sombre sky showed scarce a star.
The night was calm, but I heard in the
        swell
    A murmur of storm, and, far away,
The muffled toll of the wrecker's bell,
    As it floated up from the outer bay.

E

And a look of hate in the waiting waves
Spoke to my soul of a place of graves.

VII.

I watched them there, as I stood at the
      wheel, —
The happy lover, the radiant bride, —
And the wasting fever of frantic pain
And jealous hatred burnt my brain;
And I felt what only demons feel,
For the man who walked by that woman's
      side. . . .
Nothing they thought of danger then,
Or the schemes and crimes of wicked men.
Lost in a wordless dream of bliss,
And consecrate with marriage kiss,
What could those innocent creatures know
Of the burning hate, the maddening woe
And the deadly purpose of blind despair,
In the heart of the fiend beside them there!

VIII.

An hour had passed — he stood alone, . . .
    I thought no creature saw the blow
That felled him, senseless as a stone,
Or heard the pitiful, low moan,
    His death-sigh, as he sank below

These very waters where they flow
Around that vengeful bell.
But joy, like grief, will vigils keep,
And love hath eyes that never sleep,
And secret tongues that tell.
She passed like some swift bolt of light,
A heavenly angel robed in white !
One dazzling gleam, one cry so shrill
That sea and sky and this lone hill
Are echoing with its anguish still —
And she had leaped into the night:
And on her murdered lover's breast
In the same wave she sunk to rest.

IX.

That moment o'er the sky
Flamed the red wrath of such a storm
As might enwreathe the avenger's form
When howling fiends defy.
No ship could live in the gale that blew,
And mine went down, with all her crew —
I only left alive :
Spurned upward out of weltering hell
To that same reef where swings the bell
That, ever since, with fateful spell
Hath drawn me by its hideous knell,
I breathed, and ceased to strive —

I, whom the lightning will not rend,
Nor waves engulf, nor death befriend,
   Nor holy father shrive ! . . .

X.

There's a lurid light in the clouds to-night,
   In the wind there's a desolate moan ;
But the waves roll soft on the sand so white,
   And break on the crags of stone ;
And the sea-gulls scream in their frolic
     flight,
   And all my dream is flown.
But, far away in the twilight gloom,
I still can hear it, the muffled boom, —
And it seems to be ringing a dead man's
     knell, —
Solemn and slow, of the wrecker's bell.

ACCOMPLICES.

BLACK rocks upon the ragged coast,
   Mutter no more our hidden crime !
I hear, far off, your sullen boast,
   But I defy you ! 'tis not time !

You cannot tell our secret yet ;
   The trusty sea must keep its dead,

And many suns arise and set
　Before that awful word is said.

For I am young; I've all the grace
　Of life, and love, and beauty now :
There's not a wrinkle on my face ;
　There's not a shadow on my brow.

I cannot bear the loathsome grave,
　I will not leave the cheerful sun !
Rave on ! in storm and midnight rave,
　For years and years, till all is done :

Till these brown locks are changed to gray ;
　Till these clear eyes are dim and old ;
Not yet, not yet the fatal day
　When all that horror must be told !

But, then — gnash all your jagged teeth,
　And howl for vengeance ! I will come ;
And that same cruel pit beneath
　Shall yawn and gulf me to my home.

To-day — forbear, nor mutter more !
　The sky is dark, and dark the sea,
And all the land, from shore to shore,
　Is hideous with your grisly glee.

PREDESTINED.

A CALM cold face as white and clear
    As marble, and as passionless :
Eyes darkly sad, that tell no fear,
    No hope, no pleasure, no distress :

A smile, that seems all o'er to sleep,
    As sleeps a sunbeam on a stone ;
A gentle voice, but soft and deep,
    And full of music, every tone :

A courtly manner, — he is true
    To social usage, and will pay
To all the world its proper due
    Of graceful, stately courtesy : —

Behold, an awful thought it is
    That such a ghastly, gaunt despair
Can wear a shape so grand as this,
    A face so noble and so fair !

For that is not a common grief
    Which tears his heart and burns his
        brain
Who feels eternity too brief
    For his tremendous trance of pain !

Whose soul endures infernal woes,
  Enchained by some infernal spell ;
Who knows not peace, but only knows
  The lurid, withering fires of hell !

—◦◦—

ORGIA.[2]

Who cares for nothing alone is free, —
Sit down, good fellow, and drink with me !

With a careless heart and a merry eye
He laughs at the world as the world goes
    by.

He laughs at power, and wealth, and fame;
He laughs at virtue, he laughs at shame ;

He laughs at hope, and he laughs at fear;
At memory's dead leaves, crisp and sere ;

He laughs at the future, cold and dim, —
Nor earth nor heaven is dear to him.

O, that is the comrade fit for me !
He cares for nothing, his soul is free ;

Free as the soul of the fragrant wine —
Sit down, good fellow, my heart is thine !

For I heed not custom, creed, nor law ;
I care for nothing that ever I saw.

In every city my cups I quaff,
And over the chalice I riot and laugh.

I laugh, like the cruel and turbulent wave ;
I laugh at the church, and I laugh at the
    grave.

I laugh at joy, and well I know
That I merrily, merrily laugh at woe ;

I terribly laugh, with an oath and a sneer,
When I think that the hour of death is
    near.

For I know that death is a guest divine,
Who shall drink my blood as I drink this
    wine.

And he cares for nothing ! a king is he —
Come on, old fellow, and drink with me !

With you I will drink to the solemn past,
Though the cup that I drain should be my
    last.

I will drink to the phantoms of love and
    truth ;
To ruined hopes and a wasted youth.

I will drink to the woman who wrought my
    woe,
In the diamond morning of long ago :

To a heavenly face, in sweet repose,
To the lily's snow and the blood of the rose ;

To the splendour, caught from orient skies,
That thrilled in the dark of her hazel eyes,—

Her large eyes, wild with the fire of the
    south, —
And the dewy wine of her warm, red mouth.

I will drink to the thought of a better time ;
To innocence, gone like a death-bell chime.

I will drink to the shadow of coming doom ;
To the phantoms that wait in my lonely
    tomb.

I will drink to my soul, in its terrible mood,
Dimly and solemnly understood :

And, last of all, to the monarch of sin,
Who scaled its rampart and reigns within.

My sight is fading — it dies away —
I cannot tell is it night or day.

My heart is burnt and blackened with pain,
And a horrible darkness crushes my brain.

I cannot see you — the end is nigh —
But we'll laugh together before I die.

Through awful chasms I plunge and fall —
Your hand, good fellow, — I die — that's all.

————◦◦•————

EREBUS.

THERE'S a mossy sunken grave,
   In the solemn land of dreams,
      All alone ;
Where the dusky branches wave
   O'er the banks of sable streams,
      With a moan :
A dull sky spans it overhead,
      Like a tomb ;
The wan stars glimmer far away
      In the gloom ;
   And a pale moon gleams
On the haunts of the dead,
Where the ghouls and the demons play.
And the souls that wander here
See each other very clear ;
And remember, — but weep not !
Remember, — but sleep not !
      Remember, — but cannot pray !

III.

LOVE AND DEATH.

III.

LOVE AND DEATH.

——◆——

LOVE AND DEATH.[2]

I.

ANGEL of Grief! thy spectral passage
   winging
   Above black waves and under moonless
   skies,
Where nevermore is heard the voice of sing-
   ing,
   Nor any light e'er falls from beauty's eyes,
   Now wave thy sable pinion where he lies
Whom to destroy thy fancy did create!
   In diamond pomp thy summons bade him
   rise,
And thine the blight that cursed his human
   state
And left him ocean-tost, forlorn, and deso-
   late.

II.

Man lives not as he would, but as he must !
    Deep in his soul the current of his doom
Runs darkly ; that this clod of fevered dust,
    Desiring heaven, and drifting to a tomb,
    Wantons in revelry, or droops in gloom,
Exults in action, falters in defeat,
    E'en as thy spirit doth its life illume,
Making its blood a torrent fierce and fleet,
Or as some stagnant pool where death and
    darkness meet.

III.

Thou didst create this being all of fire,
    But 'twas not all from heaven ; the grosser
    flame
Glowed with the finer, — till his mad desire
    Revelled in wild delights, contemning
    shame
    And staining the white crest of noble
    fame :
Yet all the while thy spirit fed his heart
    With wildering dreams and hopes, till he
    became
A soul of thy dark strain, and dwelt
    apart, —
The visionary child of genius and of art.

IV.

From earliest youth his spirit kept its throne
   By the sea's marge, or on the mountain
      height,
Or in the forest deeps, or meadow lone,
   Where the long shadows fall, as comes
      the night,
   And spectral shapes gleam on the startled
      sight
And vanish with low sighs: the darkling
   caves
   That line the murm'rous shore were his
      delight,
Where the defeated billow chafes and raves,
And much he loved the stars that shine on
   lonely graves.

V.

By night he roamed along the haunted
   shore,
   And on the vacant summit of the hills
Held converse with the vast; while ever-
   more
   The awful mystery with which nature
      thrills, —
   Whispering the poet's heart, and thence
      distils

The essence of her beauty, — wrapt his soul,
   Buoyant and glorious, with such power
      as fills
The dread expanse where sky and ocean
   roll,
Thought measureless, supreme, and feeling
   past control.

VI.

Among the haunts of men a wanderer still,
   He walked a dusky pathway, all his own ;
For men were not his mates — their good,
   their ill
   Were things by him unfelt, to him un-
      known —
An empty laughter or an idle moan ;
And they that saw him passed him coldly by,
   And thus he roved his shadowy world
      alone, —
A world of haunting shapes and phantasy,
And life a dream that longed yet dreaded
   more to die.

VII.

This is the bitter close — that in their flow,
   The stern years ravage from us, one by
      one,

Each hope that sanctifies a life of woe,
  All that is fair and bright beneath the
    sun,
  And that sweet faith with which our days
    begun ;
Till not one glimmering ray from heavenly
    spheres,
  O'er longings thwarted and high aims un-
    done,
Gilds the bleak stream of those remorseless
    years,
And quenched the spring of joy, and dried
    the fount of tears.

VIII.

Close, close around us draws the prison
    shade
  And ever closer, as our moments glide —
The iron web of doom ourselves have made,
  By fealty to the power which doth reside
  Within ourselves, not once to be denied,
Nor curbed, nor conquered ! Action doth
    but make
  A past to be remembered ; and the pride
Of mightiest will that would life's guidance
    take
Must, like the frailest heart, at last repine
    and break.

F

IX.

This fate was his — but not in darkness all
  Ran the wild current of his days and
    deeds;
Still on the ruined fane the moonlight falls,
  And still the radiant dawn the night suc-
    ceeds,
  And his the gentlest heart that soonest
    bleeds,
And thus the first to love and to be blest
  With that great glory of all human needs
Which, whether crowned or martyred, still
    is best —
The angel regnant once within the human
    breast.

X.

To love and to be loved — to have the bliss,
  The perfect heaven of one responsive
    soul;
To feel the throbbing heart, the burning
    kiss,
  When thought and feeling, loosed from all
    control,
  Like torrents to the sea tumultuous roll,
And life becomes all rapture — this he knew!
  And, knowing this, however fate may dole
Her mercies forth, the many or the few,
No flower is left to bloom that e'er in Eden
    grew.

XI.

He loved — he lost — and from that fatal
　　hour
　　His soul was haunted by one heavenly
　　　face ;
One sacred name had evermore the power
　　To shed a glory upon every place
　　And gild each moment with a deathless
　　　grace ! —
His heart had worshipped and his quest had
　　found,
　　And now, though cold and empty his
　　　embrace,
His lonely footsteps fell on holy ground,
With angel shapes and tones forever circling
　　round.

XII.

The dying light of sunset ; the low sigh
　　Of whispering winds that stir the faller
　　　leaves ;
The golden host of stars ; the midnight sky ;
　　The mystic sea, that not exults nor grieves ;
　　The rosy magic of the dawn that weaves
Its web of beauty, fading while it grows, —
　　All that they mean the hallowed heart
　　　receives,

Sealed with the sacrament that grief be-
    stows,
And all that nature has of tender mystery
    knows.

XIII.

Angel of Sorrow! though thy fevered hand
    Drop on the stricken heart a cross of fire ;
Though gloom and sighs and tears, a grisly
    band,
    Watch round his midnight couch till hope
      expire ;
    Though faith give o'er, and heavenly
      patience tire,
And naught remain but bitter, bleak despair,
    Yet dost thou lift thy hapless victim
      higher ! —
With nothing left to lose, he all may dare !
Who scorns the dart of death heeds not the
    frown of care !

XIV.

His o'er-fraught bosom and his haunted
    brain
    Gave out their music and then ceased to
      be —
A strange, a weird, a melancholy strain,
    Like the low moaning of the distant sea !

And when death harshly set his spirit free
From frenzied days and penury and blight,
  At least 'twas tender mercy's kind de-
      cree, —
Shrining his name in memory's living light,
With thoughts that gild the day and charm
  the lingering night.

XV.

He was the voice of beauty and of woe,
  Passion and mystery and the dread un-
      known ;
Pure as the mountains of perpetual snow,
  Cold as the icy winds that round them
      moan,
  Dark as the caves wherein earth's thun-
      ders groan,
Wild as the tempests of the upper sky,
  Sweet as the faint, far-off, celestial tone
Of angel whispers, fluttering from on high,
And tender as love's tear when youth and
  beauty die.

XVI.

Oh, if he sinned he suffered ! Let him rest,
  Who, in this world, had little but its pain !
The life of patient virtue still is blest —
  But there be bosoms powerless to restrain

The surging tempests of the heart and
    brain ;
Souls that are driven madly o'er the deep,
    Their passions fatal and their struggle
    vain ;
Men that in nameless grief their vigils keep,
With marble lips, and eyes that burn but
    cannot weep.

XVII.

Far from the blooming field and fragrant
    wood,
    The shining songster of the summer sky,
O'er ocean's black and frightful solitude
    Driven on broken wing, must sink and die;
    So on the ocean of eternity,
Far from man's help and all things bright
    and warm,
    Broken and lost, but with no lingering
    sigh —
For death, at last, is peace — his ravaged
    form
Sank in the weltering wave, and no more
    felt the storm.

XVIII.

His music dies not — nor can ever die —
    Blown round the world by every wander-
    ing wind.

The comet, lessening in the midnight sky,
   Still leaves its trail of glory far behind.
   Death cannot quench the lustre of the
      mind,
Nor hush the seraph song that beauty sings ;
   Still in the poet's soul must nature find
Her voice for every secret that she brings,
To all that dwell beneath the brooding of
   her wings.

XIX.

The silent waves of time's eternal sea
   Roll o'er the silent relics of the dead ;
But, wafted on those waters, wide and free,
   How bright, how fleet his starry songs are
      sped !
   Black gleams the deep beneath, but over-
      head
All heaven is glorious with its orbs of light,
   While, like a spirit loosed from ocean's
      bed,
Lo ! one clear echo, sounding through the
   night,
Floats up the crystal slopes of life's far
   mountain-height.

IV.

PANSIES AND ROSEMARY.

IV.

PANSIES AND ROSEMARY.

—◆—

AFTER LONG YEARS.

Dear heart, and true, in the seasons fled,
Has the world swept by me, and left me
  dead?

Have the pansies withered, I used to know?
Are the roses faded, of long ago?

Do the tapers glimmer, that lit the feast?
Has the pageant passed? has the music
  ceased?

And, musing here on the sea-beat coast,
Am I living man, or a wandering ghost?

Still in the scent of the autumn air
I feel a rapture that's like despair:

The starlight, pale on the sleeping sea,
Is a nameless, sorrowful joy to me:

And, lit by orb or crescent of night,
Meadow and woodland are brave to sight.

Still I bend to the mystic power
Of the strange sea-breeze and the breath of
    flower;

And the face of beauty wakes the wraith
Of holy passion and knightly faith !

But, ever I hear an undertone —
A subtle, sorrowful, wordless moan;

The dying note of a funeral bell;
The faltering sigh of a last farewell:

And ever I see, through lurid haze,
The sombre phantoms of other days;

In light that's sad as the ruin it frets, —
The solemn light of a sun that sets.

Ah, never now does youth dream on
As it used to dream in the summers gone !

For round it dashes the tide of years;
Its eyes are darkened with mist of tears;

Its hopes are sere as the fading grass,
And nothing it wished has come to pass.

Yet ever, in wayward, passionate power,
Like a wind that moans through a ruined
    tower,

O'er memory's darkening fields along
It rustles the fallen leaves of song :

And, wild in the heart, it wakes the thrill
That nothing but death can ever still !

THE HARBINGER.

I.

ORDAINED to work the heavenly will
    Comes a bright angel, sent from far ;
And nature feels another thrill,
    And love has lit another star.

II.

Earth was more beautiful because of him.
        Wild flowers were born ;
    And limpid, bickering brooks,
    The poet's earliest books,
    Spoke of a new delight
        Unto the morn :

And, in the fragrant night,
When fairies, sporting underneath the moon,
In airy glee
And revelry,
Make the wide darkness beautifully bright,
Like brightest noonday in the heart of June,
Every billow laughed, and after
Seemed to chase its nimble laughter;
Till spent,
With emulous merriment,
It sunk to sleep in some secluded, cool,
And black and lucent pool.

III.

On meadows starred with daisies
The wild bee swooned, in mazes
Of witching odour, richer far
Than spikenard, rose, and jasmine are.
All natural objects seemed to catch a rare
and precious gleam.
Unknowing why, the happy birds
Trilled out their hearts in seeming joyous
words,
All indistinct, though sweet, to mortal
ears;
Such as a poet hears,
With joy and yet with tears,

In some ethereal reverie, half vision and
  half dream.
Through breezy tree-tops jocund voices
  thrilled,
And, deep in slumberous caverns of the
  ocean,
Wild echo heard, and with an airy
  motion
Tossed back the greeting of a heart o'er-
  filled
With gladness, and that speaks it o'er and
  o'er,
      Till bliss can say no more.
The waves that whispered on the listening
  sands
Told the glad tidings unto many lands,
And the stars heard, and from their wandering isles
Dropt down the blessing of their golden
  smiles.

IV.

Touched by the lightning of the Maker's eyes
    He spake in prophecies,
Interpreting the earth, the sea, the skies —
    All that in nature is of mystery,
        And that in man is dark,
    All that the perfect future is to be,

When quenched our mortal spark
And souls imprisoned are at last set free.
Backward he gazed, across the eternal sea,
And on the ever-lessening shores of time
Saw ghosts of ruined empires wandering
slow.
Then, onward looking, saw the radiant
bow
Of promise, shining o'er a heavenly clime.
And thus he knew of life its mystic truth—
Hope, with perpetual youth,
And that wherein all doubt and trouble
cease,
Sweet child of patience, peace.

v.

And now came death, a gentle, welcome
guest,
And touched his hand and led him into
rest.
Time paid its tribute to eternity —
A great soul, ripe for the immortal day —
And earth embraced his ashes: cold their
bed,
For now the agéd year was also dead.
The winter wind shrieked loud, with hoarse
alarms,
The keen stars shivered in the midnight
air,

And the bare trees stretched forth their
    stiffened arms
To the wan sky, in pale and speechless
    prayer.

VI.

Speak softly here, and softly tread,
    For all the place is holy ground
Where nature's love enshrines her dead,
    And earth with blessing folds them round.

He rests at last : the world far-off
    May riot in her mad excess,
But now her plaudit and her scoff
    To him alike are nothingness.

He learned in depths where virtue fell,
    The heights to which the soul may rise :
He sounded the abyss of hell,
    He scaled the walls of paradise.

What else ?   Till every wandering star
    In heaven's blue vault be cold and dim,
Our faithful spirits, following far,
    Walk in the light that falls from him.

—◦◦—

HOMEWARD BOUND.

On roseate shores, in evening's glow,
    With pulsing music soft and sweet,

G

While winds of summer gently blow,
　　The waves of time's great ocean beat;
No cloud obscures the heavenly dome,
　　And only on the shining sea
The tossing crests of silver foam
　　Presage the tempest yet to be.

Low down upon the ocean's verge,
　　Blent with the waters and the skies,
Far, far across the sounding surge,
　　The golden city's towers arise:
Fair in the sunset light they gleam,
　　Youth's chosen realm, bold manhood's
　　　　goal,
The promised land of fancy's dream,
　　The golden city of the soul!

How softly bright, how purely cold,
　　Those domes and pinnacles of bliss!
How radiant, through its gates of gold,
　　That world of rapture smiles on this!
How glorious, in the dying day,
　　O'er bastion ridge and glimmering moat,
Through rainbow clouds and rosy spray,
　　Its purple banners flash and float!

There, safe from every mortal ill,
　　Waits every wasted wish of man;

The hopes that time could ne'er fulfil,
　And only death and nature can !
There peace shall touch the eyes of grief,
　And mercy soothe the heart of pain ;
And every bud, and flower, and leaf
　That withered here shall bloom again !

Ah, sailor to the golden realm,
　With hope's glad haven clear before,
Why muse beside the idle helm,
　With listless glances back to shore ?
Night hovers o'er his trackless way,
　To blot the stars and dim the laud ;
What voice is at his heart, to stay
　The signal wafture of his hand ?

Not thus, in other days, his soul
　Of power and trust could wander back —
But saw the mists of time unroll,
　And angels throng the shining track ;
Heard mystic voices, from afar,
　Of warders on the sacred coast ;
Sprang up to meet the morning star
　And mingle with the heavenly host.

But he has borne the rage of storms,
　Through many a slow and patient year,
Still following those celestial forms
　That beckon and elude him here :

Till doubt has dimmed his eager gaze,
  And toil subdued his ardent mind,
And sorrow burdened all his days
  With quest of peace he could not find.

Her kiss is cold upon his lips,
  Who swore to be forever true ;
His eyes have seen youth's phantom ships
  Fade down beyond the distant blue ;
His hand has cleared the gathering moss
  From many a tablet, cold and white,
Where, dark with sense of doom and loss,
  His comrades sleep, in starless night.

The wayward shafts of cruel fate,
  That strike the best and purest lives ;
The curse of blessings come too late ;
  The broken faith that life survives ;
Love's frail pretence, ambition's lure,
  Malignant envy's poisoned dart,
That wounds and tortures, past a cure,
  The mangled, seared, embittered heart ;—

The weary, wistful, sad repose
  Of ardour quenched and feeling sped ;
The arid calm he only knows
  Whose hope is — like his idols — dead ;
All that repentant spirits bear,
  For sin and folly past recall ;

Remorse, endurance, patience, care —
  His soul has known and borne them all.

Ah, touch him gently, winds of night,
  And ocean odours, vague and strange,
Revive his morn of young delight —
    Supreme o'er doubt, and fear, and
      change !
The fading tints of life restore,
  The wasted fires of youth relume,
And round his radiant path once more
  Let music sound and roses bloom !

Long has he gazed in nature's eyes,
  Long kept the faith her glory yields, —
The pageant of the starry skies,
  The flowery pomp of spangled fields,
The fragrant depth of woodland ways,
  White in the moon, or dusk and dim,
And lonely mountain tops that blaze
  Through sunset lustre, vast and grim.

Long has he bowed at nature's shrine —
  Shall nature's soul desert him now ?
Ah ! shine again, thou star divine,
    And touch with light his darkening
      brow !
Though pleasures pall, though idols fall,
  Though wisdom end in long regret,

Death's glorious conquest pays for all,
    And He who made will not forget ! . . .

The day is done, the storm is free,
    And night and danger ride the gale ;
But, bravely speeding, far at sea,
    Gleams, white and clear, a lessening sail !
One moment seen, now lost to sight,
    'Mid driving cloud and ocean's roar ;
But, steered by Mercy's beacon-light,
    He yet shall reach the golden shore.

BEAUTY.

I HAD a dream, one glorious, summer night,
In the rich bosom of imperial June.
Languid I lay upon an odorous couch,
Golden with amber, festooned wildly o'er
With crimson roses ; and the longing stars
Wept tears of light upon their clustered
    leaves.
Above me soared the azure vault of heaven,
Vast and majestic ; cinctured with that
    path
Whereby, perchance, the sea-born Venus
    found

Her way to higher spheres ; that path which
    seems
A coronet of silver, gemmed with stars,
And bound upon the forehead of the night.
There, as I lay, the musical south wind
Shook all the roses into murmurous life,
And poured their fragrance o'er me, in a
    shower
Of crimson mist ; and softly, through the
    mist,
Came a low, sweet, enchanting melody,
A far-off echo from the land of dreams,
Which with delicious languor filled the air,
And steeped in bliss the senses and the
    soul.
Then rose a shape, a dim and ghostly shape,
Whereto no feature was, nor settled form,
A shadowy splendour, seeming as it came
A pearly summer cloud, shot through and
    through
With faintest rays of sunset ; yet within
A spirit dwelt ; and, floating from within,
A murmur trembled sweetly into words : —
I am the ghost of a most lovely dream,
Which haunted, in old days, a poet's mind.
And long he sought for, wept, and prayed
    for me ;
And searched through all the chambers of
    his soul,

And searched the secret places of the earth,
The lonely forest and the lonely shore ;
And listened to the voices of the sea,
What time the pale stars shone, and mid-
    night cold
Slept on the dark waves whispering at his
    feet ;
And sought the mystery in a human form,
Amid the haunts of men, and found it not ;
And looked in woman's fond, bewildering
    eyes,
And mirrored there his own, and saw no
    sign :
But only in his sleep I came to him,
And gave him fitful glimpses of my face,
Whereof he after sang, in sweetest words ;
Then died, and came to me. But evermore,
Through lonely days and passion-haunted
    nights,
A life of starlight gloom, do poets seek
To rend the mystic veil that covers me,
And evermore they grasp the empty air.
For only in their dreams I come to them,
And give them fitful glimpses of my face,
And lull them, siren-like, with words of
    hope —
That promise, sometime, to their ravished
    eyes,

Beauty, the secret of the universe,
The thought that gives the soul eternal
peace.

Then the voice ceased, and only, through
the mist,
The shaken roses murmured, and the wind.

LETHE.

I.

SWEET oblivion, blood of grape,
Let me take thy hue and shape !
Flood this heavy heart of mine !
Turn it into ruddy wine !
Through my veins, with golden glow,
Airy spirit, flash and flow !
Deify this clod of clay !
Waft my willing soul away !

II.

Dark and sad my fancies are —
Tired of peace and tired of war.
Joke of jester, prank of clown,
Weigh my heavy eyelids down.

All philosophies are drear;
Music's jargon in my ear;
Endless tides of empty talk
Bubble round me where I walk;
I am deafened by the din
That the world is wrangling in.

III.

Prince of sunrise, fiery wine,
Let me lose my soul in thine!
Close my eyes and stop my tears
To all a mortal sees or hears: —
Roll of drums, and clash of swords,
Fretful snarl of angry words,
Church, and state, and bond, and free,
Party, creed, and policy,
Tattle, prattle, laugh, and groan,
Crozier, sceptre, flag, and throne,
Garrulous and grand debate
Which of moles is small or great,
Whom to pray for, who shall pray,
And what agile critics say.

IV.

Sun of rubies, radiant wine,
Melt my being into thine!
So my dream of death shall bless
Memory with forgetfulness.

No more weary, wasting thought
On a past so folly-fraught!
No more dreams of love-lit eyes,
Silken hair and tender sighs,
And wild kisses sweet, that shake
The frame of being! — poor mistake!
Nor that other, just as poor, —
Toil for praise of sage or boor;
Fire, that burnishes a crown,
Fire, that burns a kingdom down,
Fire, that ravages his breast,
Who takes ambition for its guest!
But at last, instead of these,
Sunset cloud and evening breeze,
Holy starlight shining dim,
Organ wail and vesper hymn,
Cypress wreath and asphodels,
Gentle toll of distant bells, —
All that makes the sleeper blest
In a bed of endless rest.

v.

When this farce of life is o'er,
Are we fretted any more?
Do they rest, I'd like to know,
Under grass or under snow,
Who have gone that silent way
You and I must go, some day?

If they do, it seems to me
Happy were it thus to be
Sleeping where the blackb'ries grow,
And the bramble-roses blow,
And the sunshine pours its gold
On mossy rock and woodland old,
While gentle winds, and clouds of fleece,
And rippling waters whisper — peace !

VI.

Vain the fancy : nothing dies :
Falling water falls to rise ;
Round and round the atoms fly, —
Turf, and stone, and sea, and sky,
Vapour-drop and blood of man, —
In the inexorable plan.
All is motion : nothing dies :
Mystery of mysteries !

VII.

Royal road of blest escape !
Sweet oblivion, blood of grape,
Let me take thy hue and shape !
In thy spirit floating free,
I shall be a reverie,
A flitting thought, a fading dream,
A melting cloud, a faint moonbeam,

A breath, a mist, a ghost of light,
To rise and vanish in the night, —
Unseeing all, by all unseen,
And being as I had not been.

THE WHITE FLAG.

I.

BRING poppies for a weary mind
  That saddens in a senseless din,
And let my spirit leave behind
  A world of riot and of sin, —
In action's torpor deaf and blind.

Bring poppies — that I may forget !
  Bring poppies — that I may not learn !
But bid the audacious sun to set,
  And bid the peaceful starlight burn ;
O'er buried memory and regret.

Then will the slumberous grasses grow
  Above the bed wherein I sleep ;
While winds I love will softly blow,
  And dews I love will softly weep,
O'er rest and silence hid below.

Bring poppies, — for this toil is vain ;
  I cannot guide the rush of life :
A stronger hand must grasp the rein,
  A stouter arm oppose the strife,
A braver heart defy the pain.

Youth was my friend, — but youth had
     wings,
  And he has flown unto the day,
And left me, in a night of things,
  Bewildered, on a lonesome way,
And careless what the future brings.

Let there be sleep ! nor any more
  The noise of useless deed or word ;
While the free spirit hovers o'er
  A sea where not a sound is heard —
A sea of dreams, without a shore.

II.

Dark Angel, counselling defeat,
  I see thy mournful, tender eyes ;
I hear thy voice, so faint, so sweet,
  And very dearly should I prize
Thy perfect peace, thy rest complete.

But is it rest to vanish hence,
  To mix with earth, or sea, or air ?

Is death indeed a full defence
  Against the tyranny of care ?
Or is it cruellest pretence ?

And, if an hour of peace draws nigh,
  Shall we, who know the arts of war,
Turn from the field and basely fly,
  Nor take what fate reserves us for,
Because we dream 'twere sweet to die ?

What shall the untried warriors do,
  If we, the battered veterans, fail ?
How strive, and suffer, and be true,
  In storms that make our spirits quail,
Except our valour lead them through ?

Though for ourselves we droop and tire,
  Let us at least for them be strong.
'Tis but to bear familiar fire ;
  Life at the longest is not long,
And peace at last will crown desire.

So, Death, I will not hear thee speak !
  But I will live and still endure
All storms of pain that time can wreak. . . .
  My flag be white because 'tis pure,
And not because my soul is weak !

THE SCEPTRE.

The dark'ning shadows eastward slope
 And evening, with her dewy urn,
Quenches the beacon orb of hope,
 To let the stars of patience burn.

The paths grow dim, the low winds sigh,
 The fluttering bird-notes faint and fail,
And slowly up the sombre sky
 The sad moon wanders, cold and pale.

Yet on for many a weary mile
 Our pilgrim marches still must wend,
Through brier and flood, by lane and stile,
 Before we reach our journey's end.

What word will cheer the jaded nerve?
 What thought inspire, as on we fare,
The baffled mind, so prone to swerve
 Beneath the leaden wings of care?

Ah, nature, when she made her toy, —
 This wayward child of fire and clay,
The sport of every fickle joy
 That ripples through his fleeting day, —

Gave him a fancy swift to breed
 Delusive dreams for every hour —

Sirens that beckon and recede,
 And phantom moods of bliss and power.

Some from the stars and flowers distil
 The faith that these not vainly shine, —
That whispering wood and rock-crowned
  hill
 And murmuring stream are all divine.

Some for a vanished love bewail —
 Her eyes, the starry orbs of fate,
And voice, more rich than summer gale,
 That make the heaven in which they wait.

Some, self-enamoured, seem so dear,
 So sacred in their own kind eyes,
They cannot doubt what blossoms here
 Must bloom again in paradise.

Some from the written lore of sage
 Evolve and shape the eternal plan ;
Some boldly vaunt the inspired page
 And claim immortal life for man.

So onward down the dark ravine, —
 Dim phantoms in a phantom night, —
We wander toward a realm unseen
 Where nothing dwells but love and light.

Vain dreams ! of mortal frailty wrought
   And nameless dread of nameless ill !
Man's sceptre is the regnant thought
   And towering calm of human will !

One lesson comes to all that live,
   One final truth their lives declare, —
That earth has nought but toil to give,
   And nought to teach but how to bear:

The chastened calm of dumb assent,
   Though hope should wither or should
      bloom,
Blind to all purpose or event,
   And silent, 'neath the eyes of doom.

This, only this, remains of all
   The morning pomp of young belief —
That man, else nature's abject thrall,
   In royal will is nature's chief.

Thought falters, faith is dazed with fear,
   Earth keeps her secret, death is dumb:
This simply bears its burden here,
   And dauntless fronts whate'er may come.

As some tall ship that braves the storm —
   Straight out to sea her prow is bent,

Where, broken on her stalwart form,
　The furies of the surge are spent:

Or, torn by rock and whelmed by wave,
　Exultant when her doom is met,
She rears above her ocean grave
And sinks with every standard set.

———◦◦———

IN A CHURCHYARD.

I.

THE lonesome wind of autumn grieves;
　The northern lights are seen ;
October sheds her changing leaves
　Upon the churchyard green,
Where, sitting pensive in the sun,
　While fading grasses wave,
I watch the crickets leap and run,
　Upon a stranger's grave.

II.

There is no sigh of fluttering leaf,
　No sob of rustling grass ;
The breezes o'er this place of grief
　In breathless whisper pass ;

Yet, like a murmur in a dream,
  Purls on that insect voice —
That vacant tone, which does not seem
  To mourn or to rejoice.

III.

A tone that hath no soothing grace,
  A tone that nothing saith,
A tone that's like this solemn place
  Of memory, tears, and death —
It darkens hope, it deepens gloom,
  Black dread and doubt profound,
Turning the silence of the tomb
  To more mysterious sound.

IV.

There's night upon the face of fame,
  There's night on beauty's eyes,
Nor pure renown nor glorious shame
  From out their ashes rise:
In vain the shrines of prayer are trod —
  Nor sound nor silence breathe
The thought that flowers upon this sod,
  The secret hid beneath.

V.

Ah, piteous, desolate, and drear
  This nameless stranger's sleep,

O'er which the slowly dying year
  Is all that seems to weep !
Ah, save him, in that bitter day, —
  His heart, his reason save, —
Who hears the crickets chirp, at play,
  Upon his darling's grave !

———◦◦◦———

BEYOND THE DARK.

THERE'S a region afar from earth
  Should be very happy to-day ;
For a sweet soul, ripe for its birth,
  Has flown from its prison away.

And I think, as I muse alone,
  While the night is falling around,
Of a cold, white, glimmering stone,
  And a desolate, grassy mound ;

Of eyes that will shine never more,
  Of hands that have finished their task ; —
And my heart is heavy and sore,
  And my thought is eager to ask

If, at last, all things will be well,
  In the morning beyond the dark ;
What secret the pale lips could tell
  Of the sleeper, silent and stark.

But there comes a murmur of trees,
  That wave their glad branches, and bring
Blossoms and leaves, to shake in the breeze,
  From miraculous spring to spring;

And they whisper that all is well,
  For the same hand is guiding us all,
Whether 'tis felt in man's death-knell,
  Or in autumn leaves as they fall.

And so many have gone before,
  That the voice of another sphere
Floats oft from o'er a sable shore,
  And pierces the shadow of fear.

O heart that forever is still,
  Thou wilt ache with trouble no more,
Nor know of the good or the ill
  Of a lunatic world's uproar!

Nor care for the great or the small
  Of a strange, bewildering life,
That oft seems dust and ashes all,
  And is mostly a vapid strife!

For the end is the peace of grass,
  And the spirit, ever to be:
One for us to feel as we pass,
  The other encompassing thee.

Clouds sail and the bright waters flow,
   And our spirits must journey on ;
But it cannot be ill to go
   The way upon which thou hast gone.

————•◦•————

THE ANGEL OF DEATH.

COME with a smile, when come thou must,
   Evangel of the world to be,
And touch and glorify this dust, —
   This shuddering dust, that now is me, —
   And from this prison set me free !

Long in those awful eyes I quail,
   That gaze across the grim profound :
Upon that sea there is no sail,
   Nor any light nor any sound
   From the far shore that girds it round :

Only — two still and steady rays
   That those twin orbs of doom o'ertop ;
Only — a tranquil, patient gaze
   That drinks my being, drop by drop,
   And bids the pulse of nature stop.

Come with a smile, auspicious friend,
   To usher in the eternal day !

Of these weak terrors make an end,
　　And charm the paltry chains away
　　That bind me to this timorous clay !

And let me know my soul akin
　　To sunrise, and the winds of morn,
And every grandeur that has been
　　Since this refulgent world was born, —
　　Nor longer droop in my own scorn.

Come, when the way grows dark and chill !
　　Come, when the baffled mind is weak,
And in the heart the voice is still,
　　That used in happier days to speak,
　　Or only whispers, sadly meek.

Come with thy smile that dims the sun,
　　Thy pitying heart and gentle hand,
To waft me, from my vigil done,
　　To peace, that waits on thy command,
　　In some yet undiscovered land.

THE SIGNAL LIGHT.

The lonely sailor, when the night
　　O'er ocean's glimmering waste descends,
Sets at the peak his signal light,
　　And fondly dreams of absent friends.

Starless the sky above him broods,
  Pathless the waves beneath him swell;
Through peril's spectral solitudes
  That beacon flares — and all is well.

So, on the wandering sea of years,
  When now the evening closes round,
I show the signal flame that cheers,
  And scan the wide horizon's bound.

The night is dark, the winds are loud,
  The black waves follow, fast and far;
Yet soon may flash, through mist and cloud,
  The radiance of some answering star.

Haply across the shuddering deep,
  One moment seen, a snowy sail
May dart with one impetuous leap,
  And pass with one exultant hail!

And I shall dearly, sweetly know,
  Though storm be fierce and ocean drear,
That somewhere still the roses blow,
  And hearts are true, and friends are near.

Each separate on the eternal main,
  We seek the same celestial shore:
Sometimes we part to meet again,
  Sometimes we part to meet no more.

Ah, comrades, prize the gracious day
  When sunshine bathes the tranquil tide,
And, careless as a child at play,
  Our ships drift onward, side by side !

Too oft, with cold and barren will,
  And stony pride of iron sway,
We bid the voice of love be still,
  And thrust the cup of joy away.

No comfort haunts the yellow leaf !
  Wait not till, broken, old, and sere,
The sad heart pines, in hopeless grief,
  For one sweet voice it used to hear.

Thought has its throne, and power its glow,
  And wealth will bless, and beauty please ;
But the best hours that life can know
  Are rose-crowned hours of mirth and ease.

Let laughter leap from every lip !
  To music turn the perfumed air !
Ye golden pennons, glance and dip !
  Ye crimson banners, flash and flare !

On them no more the tempest glooms
  Whose freed and royal spirits know
To frolic where the lilac blooms
  And revel where the roses blow !

But, lights of heaven above them kiss,
　　As over silver seas they glide —
One heart, one hope, one fate, one bliss —
　　To peace and silence, side by side.

SYMBOLS.

Not only to give light those urns
　　Of golden fire adorn the skies !
Not for her vision only burns
　　The glory of a woman's eyes !
But in those flames and that fine glance
Th' authentic flags of heaven advance.

In them we know our life divine,
　　For which th' unnumbered planets roll !
Action and suffering are but sign :
　　Within the shadow dwells the soul ;
And till we rend this earthly thrall
We do not truly live at all.

ASHES.

[WRITTEN IN THE SHAKESPEARE CHURCH AT STRAT-
FORD-UPON-AVON.]

No eyes can see man's destiny completed
　　Save His, who made and knows th' eter-
　　　　nal plan :

As shapes of cloud in mountains are re-
    peated,
  So thoughts of Fate accomplished are in
    man.

Here the divinest of all thoughts descended ;
  Here the sweet heavens their sweetest
    boon let fall ;
Upon this hallowed ground begun and ended
  The life that knew, and felt, and uttered
    all.

There is not anything of human trial
  That ever love deplored or sorrow knew,
No glad fulfilment and no sad denial,
  Beyond the pictured truth that Shake-
    speare drew.

All things are said and done, and though
    forever
  The streams dash onward and the great
    winds blow,
There comes no new thing in the world, and
    never
  A voice like his, that seems to make it so.

Take then thy fate, or opulent or sordid,
  Take it and bear it and esteem it blest ;
For of all crowns that ever were awarded
  The crown of simple patience is the best.
    1889.

THE PASSING BELL AT STRATFORD.

[IT IS A TRADITION IN STRATFORD-UPON-AVON THAT
THE BELL OF THE GUILD CHAPEL WAS TOLLED AT
THE DEATH AND FUNERAL OF SHAKESPEARE.]

SWEET bell of Stratford, tolling slow,
In summer gloaming's golden glow,
I hear and feel thy voice divine,
And all my soul responds to thine.

As now I hear thee, even so,
My Shakespeare heard thee long ago,
When lone by Avon's pensive stream
He wandered, in his haunted dream:

Heard thee — and far his fancy sped
Through spectral caverns of the dead,
And strove — and strove in vain — to pierce
The secret of the universe.

As now thou mournest didst thou mourn
On that sad day when he was borne
Through the green aisle of honied limes,
To rest beneath the chambered chimes.

He heard thee not, nor cared to hear !
Another voice was in his ear,

And, freed from all the bonds of men,
He knew the awful secret then.

Sweet bell of Stratford, toll, and be
A sacred promise unto me
Of that great hour when I shall know
The path whereon his footsteps go.

Written at Stratford, September 14, 1890.

HEAVEN'S HOUR.

[WRITTEN ON HEARING ORGAN MUSIC AT NIGHT IN
SHAKESPEARE'S CHURCH AT STRATFORD, SEPTEM-
BER 18, 1890.]

CAN I forget ? — no, never while my soul
Lives to remember — that imperial night
When through the spectral church I heard
    them roll,
Those organ tones of glory, and my sight
Grew dim with tears, while ever new delight
Throbbed in my heart, and through the
    shadowy dread
The pale ghosts wandered, and a deathly
    chill
Froze all my being — the mysterious thrill
That tells the awful presence of the dead !

Yet not the dead, but, strayed from heav-
    enly bowers,
Pure souls that live with other life than
    ours :
For sure I am that ecstasy of sound
Lured one sweet spirit from his holy
    ground,
Who dwells in the perpetual land of flowers.

----•••----

THE MERRY MONARCH.

It comes into my mind, in a genial mood,
    When the worlds of my being, without
        and within,
Are pensively happy, in all that is good,
    Unclouded by care and untempted by
        sin, —
If the gods would but grant me my dearest
    desire,
    As sometimes I think them propitious to
        do,
That I shouldn't sit here, looking into the
    fire,
    And dreaming, my love, as I'm dreaming
        of you.

Nor should I be thinking, as sometimes I
 am, —
 If the gods had but made me the thing I
  would be, —
That a station of rank, in a world full of
 sham,
 Were a pleasant and suitable station for
  me.
Nor would ever a fancy drift into my brain
 For the laurel that bards are so wishful
  to wear, —
That dubious guerdon for labour and pain,
 That sorry exchange for the natural hair.

No! I never should care, if I had my own
 way,
 For the storm or the sunshine, the yes or
  the no ;
But, merrily careless and perfectly gay,
 I could let the world go as it wanted to
  go.
I should ask neither riches, nor station, nor
 power ;
 They are chances, they happen, and there
  is an end ;
But a heart that beats happily every hour
 Is a god's richest gift, is a man's truest
  friend.

And that's what I'd have !   For that bless-
    ing I pray !
A spirit so gentle and easy and bright,
It would gladden with sunshine the sunni-
    est day,
    And with magical splendour illumine the
        night.
I could envy no potentate under the sun,
    However sublime might that potentate be !
For I'd live, the illustrious monarch of fun,
    And the rest of the world should be happy
        with me.

I'd be gold in the sunshine and silver in
    showers ;
    I'd be rainbows, and clouds all of purple
        and pearl ;
And the fairies of fun should laugh out of
    the flowers,
    And the jolly old earth should be all in a
        whirl !
The brooks should trill music, the leaves
    dance in glee,
    And old ocean should bellow with surly
        delight :
O, but wouldn't it be a rare pageant to see,
    If the gods did but grant me my kingdom
        to-night !

I

And I think it will come, — that succession
    of mine,
  That crown with the opals of jollity set;
And the joy in my soul will be almost
    divine
  When I finally teach myself how to for-
    get;
Forget every trouble in which I've a part,
  All the dreams that allure and the hopes
    that betray;
Contented to wait, with a right merry heart,
  For silence and night and the end of the
    play.

BLUE AND BLACK.

I.

HERE's a health to the lass with the merry
  black eyes !
  Here's a health to the lad with the blue
    ones !
Here's a bumper to love, as it sparkles and
  flies,
  And here's joy to the hearts that are true
    ones !
Yes, joy to the hearts that are tender and
  true, —

With a passion that nothing can smother !
To the eyes of the one, that are pensive and
    blue,
And the merry black eyes of the other !

II.

Mind this now, my lad, with the sweet eyes
    of blue,
That, whatever the graces invite you,
There is nothing for you in this world that
    will do
But a pair of black eyes to delight you :
And mind, my gay lass, with the dear eyes
    of black,
In a pair of blue eyes to discover
That pure light of affection you never should
    lack, —
And you'll always be true to your lover !

III.

Long, long shall your eyes sparkle back
    with a kiss
To the eyes that live but to behold you :
Long, long shall the magic of mutual bliss
    In a heaven of rapture enfold you !
And forever to you shall that singer be wise,
    Whose sweet thought is the truest of true
      ones, —

That the answering lustre of merry black
  eyes
Is the life of a pair of true blue ones.

AN EMPTY HEART.

[WITH A HEART-SHAPED JEWEL-BOX.]

I.

WELL, since our lot must be to part
  (These lots — how they do push and pull
    one !)
I send you here an empty heart,
  But send it from a very full one.
My little hour of joy is done,
  But every vain regret I smother,
With murm'ring, ' When you see the one,
  Think kindly sometimes of the other.'

II.

This heart must always do your will,
  This heart your maid can fetch and carry,
This heart will faithful be, and still
  Will not importune you to marry.
That other, craving hosts of things,
  Would throb and flutter, every minute ;
But this, except it hold your rings,
  Will mutely wait with nothing in it.

III.

Oh, happy heart! that finds its bliss
　In pure affection consecrated!
But happier far the heart, like this,
　That heeds not whether lone or mated;
That stands unmoved in beauty's eyes,
　That knows not if you leave or take it,
That is not hurt though you despise,
　And quite unconscious when you break it.

IV.

That other heart would burn and freeze,
　And plague, and hamper, and perplex you,
But this will always stand at ease,
　And never pet and never vex you.
Go, empty heart! and if she lift
　Your little lid this prayer deliver:
'Ah, look with kindness on the gift,
　And think with kindness on the giver.'

THE NIGHT WIND.

The night-wind that sobs in the trees—
Ah, would that my spirit could tell
What an infinite meaning it breathes,
What a sorrow and longing it wakes!

Stronachlacher, September 1, 1890.

NEVER.

THE sere leaves rustle in the moaning blast,
The dreary rain is pattering on the roof,
Sad bells, far off, toll through the twilight
  hours —
 And I shall never see thy face again !

The shadows deepen, but there comes no
  dawn ;
And through the dark I hear the rustling
  robe
Of the grim angel that has veiled my eyes —
 Never to see thy glorious face again !

V.

AT VESPER TIME.

V.

AT VESPER TIME.

AT ANCHOR.

I.

WHILE pale with rage the wild surf springs
    Athwart the harbour bar,
The safe ships fold their snowy wings,
    Beneath the evening star:
In this calm haven rocked to sleep,
    All night they swing and sway,
Till mantles o'er the morning deep
    The golden blush of day.

II.

Here, safe from every storm of fate,
    From worldly strife and scorn,
Thus let me fold my hands and wait
    The coming of the morn;
While all night long, o'er moon-lit turf,
    The wind brings in from far
The moaning of the baffled surf
    Athwart the harbour bar.

137

IN PEACE.

I.

GREEN trees and grassy fields and sunset
        light,
    With holy silence, save for rippling leaves
And birds that twitter of the coming night,
    Calling their mates, beneath my cottage
        eaves —
These Fate hath granted for a little space
    To be companions of my pilgrimage,
Filling my grateful heart with nature's grace.

II.

Not unremembered here life's garish stage,
    Nor the wild city's uproar, nor the race
For gain and power, in which all lives en-
        gage ;
    But here remembered dimly, in a dream,
As something fretful that hath ceased to
        fret —
    Now, when time lapses like a gentle
        stream,
Hid in the woodland's heart, and I forget
    To note its music and its silver gleam.

III.

But never, never let me cease to know,
    O whispering woods and daisy-sprinkled
        grass,

The beauty and the peace that you bestow,
  When the wild fevers of ambition pass,
And the worn spirit, in its gloom and grief,
  Jinks on your bosom and there finds relief !

———•◦•———

THE GOLDEN SILENCE.

WHAT though I sing no other song ?
  What though I speak no other word ?
Is silence shame ?   Is patience wrong ? —
  At least one song of mine was heard :

One echo from the mountain air,
  One ocean murmur, glad and free —
One sign that nothing grand or fair,
  In all this world was lost to me.

I will not wake the sleeping lyre ;
  I will not strain the chords of thought ;
The sweetest fruit of all desire
  Comes its own way, and comes unsought.

Though all the bards of earth were dead,
  And all their music passed away,
What nature wishes should be said
  She'll find the rightful voice to say !

Her heart is in the shimmering leaf,
 The drifting cloud, the lonely sky,
And all we know of bliss or grief
 She speaks, in forms that cannot die.

The mountain peaks that shine afar,
 The silent stars, the pathless sea,
Are living signs of all we are,
 And types of all we hope to be.

EGERIA.

THE star I worship shines alone,
 In native grandeur set apart;
Its light, its beauty, all my own,
 And imaged only in my heart.

The flower I love lifts not its face
 For other eyes than mine to see;
And, having lost that sacred grace,
 'Twould have no other charm for me.

The hopes I bear, the joys I feel,
 Are silent, secret, and serene;
Pure is the shrine at which I kneel,
 And purity herself my queen.

I would not have an impious gaze
  Profane the altar where are laid
My hopes of nobler, grander days,
  By heaven inspired, by earth betrayed.

I would not have the noontide sky
  Pour down its bold, obtrusive light
Where all the springs of feeling lie,
  Deep in the soul's celestial night.

Far from the weary strife and noise,
  The tumult of the great to-day,
I guard my own congenial joys,
  And keep my own sequestered way.

For all that world is cursed with care ;
  Has nothing holy, nothing dear,
No light, no music anywhere, —
  It will not see, it will not hear.

But thou, sweet spirit, viewless power,
  Whom I have loved and trusted long, —
In pleasure's day, in sorrow's hour, —
  Muse of my life and of my song ;

Breathe softly, thou, with peaceful voice,
  In my soul's temple, vast and dim !
In thy own perfect joy rejoice,
  With morning and with evening hymn !

And though my hopes should round me fall
　Like rain-drops in a boundless sea,
I will not think I lose them all
　While yet I keep my trust in thee !

———◆———

MY PALACES.

THEY rose in beauty on the plains
　Through which my childhood danced in
　　glee,
When roses wreathed my idle chains,
　And holy angels talked with me.

They rose sublime on mountain heights
　Whereto my ardent youth aspired, —
Through silver days and golden nights,
　Ere yet my heart grew dull and tired.

Their stately towers were all aflame
　With rosy hues of morning light ;
For hope, and love, and power, and fame
　Burned on their peaks and made them
　　bright.

Now brown and level fields expand
　Around me, as I hold my way
Through barren hills on either hand,
　And under skies of sober gray.

No radiant towers in distance rise,
   On soaring mountains strong and glad ;
No gorgeous banners flaunt the skies, —
   But all the scene is calm and sad.

Yet here and there, along the plain,
   A flower lights up the fading grass ;
And whispering wind and rustling rain
   Make gentle music as I pass.

And now and then a happy face,
   And now and then a cheerful thought
Give to the scene a pensive grace,
   The sweeter that it comes unsought.

And, looking past all earthly ill,
   I dimly see my place of rest, —
A lowly palace, dark and still,
   And sacred to the weary guest.

OLD DAYS AND LOVES.

Rosy days of youth and fancy,
   Happy hours of long ago !
Ah, the flickering sunbeam visions—
   How they waver to and fro !

Galaxies of blue-eyed Marys,
   With a Julia and a Jane,
And a troop of little Lauras,
   Blush, and laugh, and romp again.

Moonlight meetings, dreamy rambles,
   In the balm of summer night,
When our hearts were full of rapture
   And our senses of delight ; —

Those remember — and remember
   How the fond stars shone above,
Keeping, in their mellow splendour,
   Watch and ward upon our love.

Youth is like a diamond dawning —
   Bold it breaks to gorgeous day ;
Heavenly fires of power and beauty
   Blaze and burn along its way.

Far within its mystic future
   Oft are solemn voices heard !
Shaped to many a stately anthem
   Floats the music of a word.

But that music, in the present,
   Droops with passion's dull decay,
Till its echo in the spirit
   Faints, and fails, and dies away.

Green be then the tender memory
   Of the past, forever sped,
So that youth may be immortal,
   Though its days and dreams are dead!

THE SEQUEL.

THE moonbeams on the water sleep,
   In breathing light;
And tender thoughts and memories keep
   My soul to-night.

Shades of sweet hours, forever gone,
   Return unsought,
And waves of mournful joy dance on
   The stream of thought.

A dreamy fragrance seems to rise
   From other years —
A solemn bliss, that dims the eyes
   With happy tears.

Life wears the glow of rosy grace
   That first it wore,
And smiles are lit on many a face
   That smiles no more.

K

The gentle friends I used to greet, —
    They all are here :
All forms are fair, all voices sweet,
    All memories dear.

All happy thoughts, all glorious dreams,
    That once were mine,
Rise, in the tender light that beams
    From auld lang syne.

But something in the heart is wrong, —
    The joyous sway,
The spirit and the voice of song
    Have died away.

These winds, that on their cloudy cars
    Sweep through the sky,
These wandering, watching, deathless stars,
    My prayer deny.

These low, sweet murmurs from the land
    And from the sea,
These waves, that kiss the silver sand,
    Speak not to me.

And not to me one voice shall speak
    For evermore,
Though the same waves in beauty break
    On the same shore.

Shine stars, sob waves, and murmur blast,
  And night-dews, weep !
To wait is left me, and at last
  The dreamless sleep.

THE NIGHT WATCH.

I.

BENEATH the midnight moon of May,
  Through dusk on either hand,
One sheet of silver, spreads the bay,
  One crescent jet the land ;
The black ships mirrored in the stream
  Their ghostly tresses shake —
When will the dead world cease to dream ?
  When will the morning break ?

II.

Beneath a night no longer May,
  Where only cold stars shine,
One glimmering ocean, spreads away
  This haunted life of mine ;
And, shattered on the frozen shore,
  My harp can never wake —
When will this night of death be o'er ?
  When will the morning break ?

THE VEILED MUSE.

Spirit of Beauty, haunt me not!
  Thou bring'st insufferable pain :
Thou, who art gone, be thou forgot,
  Nor rise to vex my rest again,
Either with memories sadly sweet,
Or hopes foredoomed to dull defeat!

Ah, come no more in rustling leaves,
  Or peaceful grass, or breath of flowers!
Enough this baffled spirit grieves,
  Remembering thee in rosy hours :
Spare it the throbs of hope and fear, —
The cruel sense that thou art near!

The passion dies within my soul ;
  The music dies within my brain ;
Save when there comes a funeral toll —
  A low, lamenting, sad refrain,
An echo from that shrine of song
Long darkened and deserted long.

In what was fair I once had part,
  But all fair things are now my shame :
Their nameless beauty hurts my heart,
  Because I cannot speak its name :

Spoken, 'twould make my soul rejoice ;
But now I cannot give it voice.

Once in these veins the blood was warm ;
  With ardent hope this heart beat high ;
And the great gales that proudly storm
  The loftiest ramparts of the sky
Were not more daring, fierce, and strong
Than this now silent soul of song.

But wasted now that youth of gold,
  Not heaven itself again could give ;
And he to die may well be bold
  Who is not bold enough to live —
In haunted silence of disgrace,
Where hushed thy voice and veiled thy
    face.

Ah, come no more to do me wrong,
  In twilight hours of tender dream,
When this worn spirit seems less strong
  Than evening mist that shrouds the
    stream.
Though love be dead, at least retain
Some pity for thy lover's pain :

Remembering still, though all be past,
  That thou and I clasped hands in youth :

I saw thee close, I held thee fast,
   Plucked kisses from thy rosy mouth —
Learning the bliss which now I weep,
The love I won but could not keep.

UNWRITTEN POEMS.

FAIRY spirits of the breeze —
Frailer nothing is than these.
Fancies born we know not where —
In the heart or in the air :
Wandering echoes blown unsought
From far crystal peaks of thought :
Shadows, fading at the dawn,
Ghosts of feeling dead and gone :
Alas ! Are all fair things that live
Still lovely and still fugitive ?

A SOUVENIR.

I.

AH, Lily, when my head lies low,
   In yonder quiet woodland dell, —
Where the wild-flowers will sweetly blow,
   Above the eyes that loved them well, —

How soon thy sorrow would depart,
If word of mine could soothe thy heart !

II.

Somewhere, some day, we meet again !
  Think this — and be this thought relief !
In life I have not brought thee pain ;
  In death I must not bring thee grief.
Strew with the flowers of hope my pall,
And gently mourn, or not at all !

———◦◇◦———

INCENSE.

TRUE heart ! upon the current of whose
    love,
My days, like roses in a summer brook,
Float by, in fragrance and in melody,
Take these — unworthy symbols of my soul,
Made precious by the heavenly faith of
    thine !
Take them : and, though a face of pain looks
    through
The marble veil of words, thy heart will
    know
That what was shadow once is sunshine
    now,

And life all peace, and beauty, and content,
Redeemed and hallowed by thy sacred
    grace.
Thrice happy he, who — favoured child of
    fate ! —
Finds his Egeria in a mortal guise,
And, hearing all the discords of the world
Blend into music, round his haunted way,
Knows hope fulfilled and bliss already won !

FULL-CIRCLE.

The future and the past are blended,
   And all will one day re-appear ;
For nothing in this world is ended,
   Whatever seems to perish here.

VI.

TRIBUTE AND COMMEMORATION.

VI.

TRIBUTE AND COMMEMORATION.

—◆—

GEORGE ARNOLD.

[Greenwood, November 13, 1865.]

Beneath the still November sky,
  With nature's peace and beauty blest,
We put our selfish sorrow by,
  And laid our comrade down to rest.

Rest — in the morning of his days !
  Rest — when his heart had just begun
To feel the warmth of rip'ning praise,
  The radiance of the rising sun !

Rest — to a strong and stately mind,
  That rose all common flights above !
Rest — to a heart as true and kind
  As ever glowed with human love !

And round him, dimly, through our grief,
  In every natural sound we heard —

In whispering grass, and rustling leaf,
  And sighing wind — the same sweet word:

Rest ! And we did not break the spell
  By holy nature woven round
The fading form we left to dwell
  Forever in her hallowed ground.

No hymns were sung, no prayers were said
  Save what our loving hearts could say,
When, mutely gazing on the dead,
  We blessed him ere we turned away:

Back to the round of daily care
  That seems so vacant to us now,
Remembering what repose was there,
  What peace, upon his marble brow.

And so we left him, — nevermore
  To see, in sunshine or in rain,
The semblance of the form he wore
  Whose loss has steeped our souls in pain.

But, long as skies of autumn smile,
  And long as clouds of autumn weep,
Or autumn leaves their splendours pile
  In sorrow o'er their poet's sleep;

And long as violets grace the spring,
  Or June-born roses blush and blow,
Or pale stars shine, or south winds sing,
  Or tides of summer ebb and flow ;

So long shall live their poet's name,
  When rest these broken hearts of ours, —
Embalmed in love, surpassing fame,
  With stars and leaves and clouds and
    flowers !

———◆◇◆———

ADA.

[DIED MARCH 4, 1874.]

SPRING will return and woods grow green
  From shore to shore ;
But she, unseeing and unseen,
  Returns no more.

Low in the ground her sleep is sweet,
  And dark, and long :
No more she treads, with wandering feet,
  Our maze of wrong.

No more the world's rebuke can fret
  Her soul's repose ;

Nor kindness woo her to forget
    Her bitter woes.

She will not stir, nor speak, nor heed,
    Though eyes that weep,
And sorrow-stricken hearts that bleed,
    Beseech her sleep.

Yet, be it mine, above her pall,
    To shed one tear,
And speak one word of love, that all
    The world may hear.

A brother's place in that fond breast
    'Twas mine to hold:
Ah, they loved most who knew her best—
    That heart of gold.

She was more kind than slumbers are
    To eyes that grieve;
And, like the constant northern star,
    Could ne'er deceive.

There was no sorrow on the earth
    But touched her heart;
And in all gentle, childlike mirth
    She bore her part.

There was no goodness but it won
    Her reverent praise ;
And full of kind deeds, simply done,
    Were all her days.

She strove, through trouble's lasting blight,
    For pathways smooth ;
And many hands she found to smite,
    And few to soothe.

A child, whom cruel want has made
    A thing forlorn,
Stretching its little hands, for aid,
    To eyes that scorn ;

And wandering through the winter night,
    For beggar's dole,
Is not more piteous in its plight
    Than was her soul.

Yet did she hope, and toil, and wait,
    Heaven's will to know,
Till came the awful stroke of fate
    That laid her low.

Sleep softly, softly, true and tried,
    Where troubles cease ;
And take at last, what life denied,
    Death's gift of peace.

JOHN BROUGHAM.

[June 4, 1874.]

If buds by hopes of spring are blessed
　That sleep beneath the snow,
And hearts by coming joys caressed,
　Which yet they dimly know, —
On fields where England's daisies gleam,
　And Ireland's shamrocks bloom,
To-day shall summer, in her dream,
　Be glad with thoughts of Brougham.

To-day, o'er miles and miles of sea,
　Beneath the jocund sun,
With merrier force and madder glee
　The bannered winds shall run :
To-day great waves shall ramp and reel,
　And clash their shields of foam,
With bliss to feel the coming keel
　That bears the wanderer home !

For he that (loved and honoured here —
　God bless his silver head !)
O'er many a heart, for many a year,
　The dew of joy has shed,

Longs for the land that gave him birth,
   Turns back to boy again,
And, bright with all the flags of mirth,
   Sails homeward o'er the main.

Ah, well may winds and waves be gay,
   And flowers and streams rejoice,
And that sweet region far away
   Become one greeting voice ;
For he draws backward to that place,
   Who ne'er, by deed or art,
Made darkness in one human face,
   Or sorrow in one heart !

He comes, whom all the rosy sprites
   That round Thalia throng
Have tended close through golden nights
   Of laughter, wit, and song ;
Whom love's bright angels still have
     known —
   He ne'er forgot to hear
The helpless widow's suppliant moan,
   Or dry the orphan's tear.

Where boughs of oak and willow toss,
   His life's white pathway flows —
With many an odour blown across,
   Of lily and of rose.

His gentle life that blessings crown
   Is fame no chance can dim ;
We honour manhood's best renown
   When now we honour him.

Grief may stand silent in the eye,
   And silent on the lip,
When, poised between the sea and sky,
   Dips down the fading ship ;
But there's one charm his heart to keep
   And hold his constant mind —
He'll find no love beyond the deep
   Like that he leaves behind !

So, to thy breast, old ocean, take
   This brother of our soul !
Ye winds, be gentle for his sake !
   Ye billows, smoothly roll !
And thou, sad Ireland, green and fair,
   Across the waters wild
Stretch forth strong arms of loving care,
   And guard thy cherished child !

And whether back to us he drift,
   Or pass beyond our view,
Where life's celestial mountains lift
   Their peaks above the blue —

His will be done whose gracious will,
   Through all our mortal fret,
The sacred blessing leaves us still, —
   To love, and not forget.

JOHN LAWRENCE TOOLE.

[AUGUST 6, 1874.]

I.

A PERFUME that all sense delights
Enchants us most on summer nights,
And music, nature's kindest boon,
Is sweetest 'neath the summer moon :
For summer night and moonlight give
Quiet and grace, in which we live ;
In which alone the prisoned soul
Finds, if not words, at least control,
And, for a moment, lifts us far
To realms where saints and angels are.
So friendship's soft and tender voice
Sounds clearest when our hearts rejoice :
For, when contentment warms the heart,
Dull thoughts and sordid cares depart —
By love exhaled — and in their place
Burns the rich glow of peace and grace.
And then we see each other clear ;
The voice within the voice we hear ;

And deep thoughts surge to eye and cheek,
Nor words, nor smiles, nor tears can speak !
The old love-ditties that were sung,
The whispered vows, when we were young,
The silken touch of fragrant tress,
The maiden's awful loveliness,
Starlight and sea-breeze, beach and spray,
The sunshine of some sacred day,
A mother's kiss on lip and brow,
The tones of loved ones, silent now,
The light that nevermore will gleam,
The broken hope, the vanished dream —
All these come thronging through the brain,
Till, half with joy and half with pain,
Our souls break loose from common things,
And soar aloft on angel wings ;
Out of the tumult and the glare,
The fretful strife, the feverish care,
To that great life of peace and grace
That waits the suffering human race ;
That larger life than sight or sound,
Wherewith great Nature folds us round. —
This is the magic, this the power,
That thrills and crowns the festal hour !

II.

'Tis summer, and the moon is bright,
And perfect gladness rules the night,
And through our rapture, gracious, free,

A silver voice, across the sea,
In tender accents whispers sweet —
' Be kind to him whom now you greet !
At England's fireside altar-stone
His fame is prized, his virtue known :
To England's heart his name is dear ;
To him she gives her smile, her tear ;
She loves him for his rosy mirth ;
She loves him for his manly worth ;
She knows him bright as morning dew ;
She knows him faithful, tender, true ;
Her hope comes with him o'er the deep, —
With him to smile, with him to weep.
Ah, give him friendship that endures,
And take him from her heart to yours.' —

III.

That voice is heard.   By deed and cheer,
We give him loyal welcome here !
In art's fair garden, where we stand,
We take him by the strong right hand ;
In friendship's cup the pledge we drain,
And bind him fast in friendship's chain.
Honour the man, whate'er his stage,
Who wields the arts to cheer the age !

IV.

Ah, comrades, if I could but say
(To point and close this humble lay)

What other voices float to me,
Across another, darker sea,
What words of cheer are wafted through
My fancy's realm, to him and you,—
A music then indeed might flow,
Should make your hearts and pulses glow.
For then would ring out, rich and deep,
The royal tones of some who sleep, —
The brilliant and the wise, too soon
Snatched from our side, in manhood's noon,
Ere genius half her vigil kept ;
For whom our hearts and morning wept:
And these a welcome, without stint, —
My feeble words can only hint, —
Should give this friend and comrade, come
So far from kindred and from home.
But, this denied, I prattle on, —
The echo, when the music's gone ;
With yet the hope that words well-meant
May find a grace for good intent,
With you, companions, tried and dear,
With him, the guest that's honoured here.
Nor will I think he views with scorn
These rhymes of welcome, lowly born ;
These wild-wood roses, faint but sweet, —
In kindness scattered at his feet.

GEORGE FAWCETT ROWE.

[AUGUST 29, 1875.]

I.

At morning, when the march began,
  And hope's strong eagle waved her wing,
Through banks of flowers the pathway ran,
  Beneath the silver skies of spring.

We heard the mountain torrents call,
  Far up among the peaks of snow ;
Our happy laughter rang through all
  The peaceful valleys spread below.

Our hearts were glad, our faces gay,
  We trod the slopes with careless glee,
And through the hill-gaps, far away,
  Hailed the blue splendour of the sea.

We knew no peril, felt no fear,
  Nor thought how swift the moments pass :
The sighing pines we did not hear,
  Nor our own footsteps on the grass.

But day wears on and night is near,
  Gray banners mingle with the gold,
Our ranks are thin, our faces drear,
  The sky is dark, the wind is cold ;

We hear the roaring of the waves
    Of that great sea to which we tend;
Our thoughts are in the wayside graves,
    And on the solemn journey's end.

No more in vain the pine-trees sigh,
    Full well their mournful note is known;
No footsteps pass unheeded by,
    No more unheeded fall our own.

No more we hear the joyous cries
    Reëchoed back from vale and hill;
The light has faded from our eyes,
    The music of our youth is still.

II.

Not all unlearned in sorrow's lore,
    My spirit, pensive, dwells apart,
And hears and heeds for evermore
    The dead leaves rustling in the heart.

Yet kindly fortune gives me grace,
    Through good and ill, through toil and
        pain,
To hold in ever fond embrace
    The cherished comrades that remain!

He, dearly prized, whose gracious fame
    Is goodness, bright beyond eclipse;

He, tried and true, whose honoured name
   Is in your hearts as on your lips ; —

He shall not, in this royal hour,
   Lack words of mine, my faith to prove ;
And, though they be not words of power,
   They shall be words of constant love.

His the light-hearted, cheery mirth —
   The snow-white bloom of blameless
      days —
Wisdom and grace and manly worth,
   An honest mind and simple ways.

His the pure thought, the spirit sweet,
   The wild-wood charm of graceful art,
The sadness and the joy that meet
   In nature's own benignant heart.

Him fortune never taught to fawn ;
   Want never sued to him in vain :
The word is spoken and is gone,
   The gentle thought and act remain.

On wings of deeds the soul must mount !
   When we are summoned from afar,
Ourselves, and not our words, will count —
   Not what we said, but what we are !

Ah, be it mine, or soon or late,
  In that great day, in that bright land,
With him as now to take my fate,
  Heart answering heart, hand clasped in
    hand!

—◦—

EDGAR POE.

[For the Dedication of a Monument to Poe,
at Baltimore, November 19, 1875.]

Cold is the pæan honour sings,
  And chill is glory's icy breath,
And pale the garland memory brings
  To grace the iron doors of death.

Fame's echoing thunder, long and loud,
  The pomp of pride that decks the pall,
The plaudit of the vacant crowd—
  One word of love is worth them all!

With dew of grief our eyes are dim:
  Ah, let the tear of sorrow start;
And honour, in ourselves and him,
  The great and tender human heart!

Through many a night of want and woe
  His frenzied spirit wandered wild,

Till kind disaster laid him low,
  And love reclaimed its wayward child.

Through many a year his fame has grown, —
  Like midnight, vast; like starlight, sweet;
Till now his genius fills a throne,
  And homage makes his realm complete.

One meed of justice, long delayed,
  One garland yet his virtues crave !
Ah, take, thou great and injured shade,
  The love that sanctifies the grave.

And may thy spirit, hovering nigh,
  Pierce the dense cloud of darkness
      through,
And know, with fame that cannot die,
  Thou hast the world's compassion too !

———◦◦◦———

THE VOICE OF THE SILENCE.[4]

[READ BEFORE THE SOCIETY OF THE ARMY OF THE
  POTOMAC, AT THE ACADEMY OF MUSIC, PHILA-
  DELPHIA, JUNE 6, 1876.]

BRIGHT on the sparkling sod to-day
  The youthful summer gleams;

The roses in the south wind play,
  The slumberous woodland dreams:
In golden light, 'neath clouds of fleece,
  'Mid bird-songs wild and free,
The blue Potomac flows, in peace,
  Down to the peaceful sea.

No echo from the stormy past
  Alarms the placid vale —
Nor cannon roar, nor trumpet blast,
  Nor shattered soldier's wail.
There's nothing left to mark the strife,
  The triumph, or the pain,
Where nature to her general life
  Takes back our lives again.

Yet, in your vision, evermore,
  Beneath affrighted skies,
With crash of sound, with reek of gore,
  The martial pageants rise:
Audacious banners rend the air,
  Dark steeds of battle neigh,
And frantic through the sulphurous glare
  Raves on the crimson fray!

Not time nor chance nor change can drown
  Your memories proud and high,
Nor pluck your star of conquest down
  From glory's deathless sky!

For evermore your fame shall bide —
  Your valour tried and true ;
And that which makes your country's pride
  May well be pride to you !

Forever in the soldier's thought
  The soldier's life returns —
Or where the trampled fields are fought,
  Or where the camp-fire burns.
For him the pomp of morning brings
  A thrill none else can know :
For him night waves her sable wings
  O'er many a nameless woe.

How often, face to face with death,
  In stern suspense he stood,
While bird and insect held their breath
  Within the ambushed wood !
Again he sees the silent hills,
  With danger's menace grim ;
And darkly all the shuddering rills
  Run red with blood, for him.

For him the cruel sun of noon
  Glares on a bristling plain ;
For him the cold disdainful moon
  Lights meadows rough with slain :
There's death in every sight he sees,
  In every sound he hears ;

And sunset hush and evening breeze
 Are sad with prisoned tears.

Again, worn out in fevered march,
 He sinks beside the track;
Again, beneath night's lonely arch,
 His dreams of home come back;
In morning wind the roses shake
 Around his cottage-door,
And little feet of children make
 Their music on the floor.

The tones that nevermore on earth
 Can bid his pulses leap
Ring out again, in careless mirth,
 Across the vales of sleep;
And where, in horrent splendour, roll
 The waves of vict'ry's tide,
The chosen comrades of his soul
 Are glorious at his side!

Forget! the arm may lose its might,
 The tired heart beat low,
The sun from heaven blot out his light,
 The west wind cease to blow;
But, while one spark of life is warm
 Within this mould of clay,
His soul will revel in the storm
 Of that tremendous day!

On mountain slope, in lonely glen,
  By fate's divine command,
The blood of those devoted men
  Has sanctified the land !
The funeral moss — but not in grief —
  Waves o'er their hallowed rest ;
And not in grief the laurel leaf
  Drops on the hero's breast !

Tears for the slave, when nature's gift
  Of all that man can be
Wastes, like the shattered spars that drift
  Upon the unknown sea !
Tears when the craven sinks at last, —
  No deed of valour done ;
But no tears for the soul that past
  When honour's fight was won !

He takes the hand of heavenly fate,
  Who lives and dies for truth !
For him the holy angels wait,
  In realms of endless youth !
The grass upon his grave is green
  With everlasting bloom ;
And love and blessing make the sheen
  Of glory round his tomb !

Mourn not for them beloved and gone !
  The cause they died to save

Rears its eternal corner-stone
  Upon the martyr's grave
Where, safe from every ill, they pass
  To slumber sweet and low,
'Neath requiems of the murmuring grass
  And dirges of the snow.

That sunset wafts its holiest kiss
  Through evening's gathering shades,
That beauty breaks the heart with bliss,
  The hour before it fades,
That music seems to merge with heaven
  Just when its echo dies,
Is nature's sacred promise given
  Of life beyond the skies !

Mourn not ! in life and death they teach
  This thought — this truth — sublime :
There's no man free, except he reach
  Beyond the verge of time !
So, beckoning up the starry slope,
  They bid our souls to live,
And, flooding all the world with hope,
  Have taught us to forgive.

No soldier spurns a fallen foe !
  No hate of human-kind
Can darken down the generous glow
  That fires the patriot mind !

But love shall make the vanquished strong
  And justice lift the ban,
Where right no more can bend to wrong
  Nor man be slave to man.

So from their silent graves they speak;
  So speaks that silent scene —
Where now the violet blossoms meek,
  And all the fields are green.
There wood and stream and flower and
     bird
  A pure content declare ;
And where the voice of war was heard
  Is heard the voice of prayer :

Once more in brother-like accord
  Our alien'd hearts unite ;
And clasp, across the broken sword,
  The hands that used to smite !
And since beside Potomac's wave
  There's nothing left but peace,
Be filled at last the open grave,
  And let the sorrow cease !

Sweet from the pitying northern pines
  Their loving whisper flows ;
And sweetly, where the orange shines,
  The palm-tree woos the rose :

M

Ah, let that tender music run
    O'er all the years to be ;
And Thy great blessing make us one —
    And make us one with Thee !

JOHN GILBERT.

[NOVEMBER 30, 1878.]

I.

WHERE, pure and pale, the starlight streams
    Far down the Alpine slope,
Still through eternal winter gleams
    The stainless flower of hope !
Undimmed by cloud, undrenched by tears,
    So may his laurel last, —
While shines o'er all his future years
    The rainbow of the past !

II.

Far, far from him the mournful hour
    That brings the final call,
And o'er his scenes of grace and power
    Fate lets the curtain fall !
And oh, when sounds that knell of worth,
    To his pure soul be given
A painless exit from the earth,
    And entrance into heaven !

A PLEDGE TO THE DEAD.

[READ BEFORE THE SOCIETY OF THE ARMY OF THE
POTOMAC, AT ALBANY, N.Y., JUNE 18, 1879.]

I.

FROM the lily of love that uncloses
   In the glow of a festival kiss,
On the wind that is heavy with roses,
   And shrill with the bugles of bliss,
Let it float o'er the mystical ocean
   That breaks on the kingdom of night —
Our oath of eternal devotion
   To the heroes who died for the right !

II.

They loved, as we love — yet they parted
   From all that man's spirit can prize ;
Left woman and child broken-hearted,
   Staring up to the pitiless skies ;
Left the tumult of youth, the rich guerdon
   Hope promised to conquer from fate ;
Gave all for the agonised burden
   Of death, for the Flag and the State.

III.

Where they roam on the slopes of the mountain
   That only by angels is trod,

Where they muse by the crystalline foun-
    tain —
The mystical, effluent God,
Are they lost in unspeakable splendour?
    Do they never look back and regret? —
Ah, the valiant are constant and tender,
    And honour can never forget!

IV.

Divine in their pitying sadness
    They grieve for their comrades of earth;
They will hear us, and start into gladness,
    And echo the notes of our mirth;
They will lift their white hands with a
    blessing
    We shall know by the tear that it brings —
The rapture of friendship confessing,
    With harps and the waving of wings

V.

In the grim and relentless upheaval
    That blesses the world through a curse, —
Still bringing the good out of evil,
    The garland of peace on the hearse! —
They were shattered, consumed, and for-
    saken,
    Like the shadows that fly from the dawn:
We may never know why they were taken,
    But we always shall feel they are gone.

VI.

If the wind that sighs over our prairies
   No longer is solemn with knells,
But lovely with flowers and fairies,
   And sweet with the calm Sabbath bells;
If virtue, in cottage and palace,
   Leads love to the bridal of pride,
'Tis because out of war's bitter chalice
   Our heroes drank deeply — and died.

VII.

Ah, grander in doom-stricken glory
   Than the greatest that linger behind,
They shall live in perpetual story,
   Who saved the last hope of mankind!
For their cause was the cause of the races
   That languished in slavery's night;
And the death that was pale on their
     faces
   Has filled the whole world with its light!

VIII.

To the clouds and the mountains we breathe
     it;
   To the freedom of planet and star;
Let the tempests of ocean enwreathe it;
   Let the winds of the night bear it far, —

Our oath, that, till manhood shall perish,
   And honour and virtue are sped,
We are true to the cause that they cherish,
   And eternally true to the dead !

OLIVER WENDELL HOLMES.

[READ AT THE ATLANTIC FESTIVAL IN COMMEMORA-
TION OF THE SEVENTIETH BIRTHDAY OF OLIVER
WENDELL HOLMES, AT BOSTON, DECEMBER 3,
1879.]

IF that glad song had ebbed away,
   Which, rippling on through smiles and
      tears,
Has bathed with showers of diamond spray
   The rosy fields of seventy years, —
If that sweet voice were hushed to-day
     What should we say ?

At first we thought him but a jest,
   A ray of laughter, quick to fade ;
We did not dream how richly blest
   In his pure life our lives were made
Till soon the aureole shone, confest,
     Upon his crest.

When violets fade the roses blow ;
   When laughter dies the passions wake :

His royal song that slept below,
  Like Arthur's sword beneath the lake,
Long since has flashed its fiery glow
  O'er all we know.

That song has poured its sacred light
  On crimson flags in freedom's van,
And blessed their serried ranks, who fight
  Life's battle here for truth and man —
An oriflamme, to cheer the right,
  Through darkest night !

That song has flecked with rosy gold
  The sails that fade o'er fancy's sea;
Relumed the storied days of old ;
  Presaged the glorious life to be ;
And many a sorrowing heart consoled
  In grief untold.

When, shattered on the loftiest steep
  The statesman's glory ever found,
That heart, so like the boundless deep,
  Broke, in the deep no heart can bound,
How did his dirge of sorrow weep
  O'er WEBSTER's sleep !

How sweetly did his spirit pour
  The strains that make the tear-drops start,

When, on the bleak New England shore,
 With Tara's harp and Erin's heart,
He thrilled us to the bosom's core
  With thoughts of MOORE !

The shamrock, green on Liffey's side,
 The lichen 'neath New England snows,
White daisies of the fields of Clyde,
 Twined ardent round old Albion's rose,
Bloom in his verse, as blooms the bride,
  With love and pride.

The silken tress, the mantling wine,
 Red roses, summer's whispering leaves,
The lips that kiss, the hands that twine,
 The heart that loves, the heart that
  grieves —
They all have found a deathless shrine
  In his rich line !

Ah well, that voice can charm us yet,
 And still that shining tide of song,
Beneath a sun not soon to set,
 In golden music flows along.
With dew of joy our eyes are wet —
  Not of regret.

For still, as comes the festal day,
 In many a temple, far and near,

The words that all have longed to say,
  The words that all are proud to hear,
Fall from his lips, with conquering sway,
    Or grave or gay.

No moment this for passion's heat,
  Nor mine the voice to give it scope,
When love and fame and beauty meet
  To crown their Memory and their Hope !
I cast white lilies, cool and sweet,
    Here at his feet.

True bard, true soul, true man, true friend !
  Ah, gently on that reverend head
Ye snows of wintry age descend,
  Ye shades of mortal night be shed !
Peace guide and guard him to the end,
    And Love defend !

A LOTOS FLOWER.

[On the Tenth Birthday of the Lotos Club,
  New York, March 27, 1880.]

I.

Though still the heart of twilight grieves,
  As evening's sun sinks low,
And sad winds stir the fallen leaves
  With songs of long ago,

No shadow grim can ever dim
   The glory of this hour,
When thus the blazing hearth we trim
   Beneath the Lotos flower.

II.

Old time may quench illusion's light,
   And dreams of youth depart,
But neither time nor truth can blight
   The sunshine of the heart —
That gentle light of pure content,
   Our sober manhood's dower,
Sweet peace and calm affection, blent
   Beneath the Lotos flower.

III.

In that dusk land of mystic dream
   Where dark Osiris sprung,
It bloomed beside his sacred stream,
   While yet the world was young;
And every secret nature told,
   Of golden wisdom's power,
Is nestled still in every fold
   Within the Lotos flower.

IV.

Here let our weary burdens fall,
   And passion's longings cease:

The gods of life have given all,
  When once they give us peace !
Black care shall vanish in a laugh,
  Forgot be beauty's bower,
When thus the loving cup we quaff,
  Beneath the Lotos flower !

———◦◦◦———

ELEGY AT ARLINGTON.

[READ IN ARLINGTON CEMETERY, WASHINGTON, D.C.,
ON DECORATION DAY, MAY 31, 1880.]

I.

IF this were all, if lost with those that per-
    ished, —
  O'er whom these winds of summer softly
    sigh, —
Our hopes were buried with the hearts we
    cherished,
  And life were nothing but to toil and die ;

What sadder scene than this that blooms
    before us,
  With nature's garlands decked, could
    earth display ?
What mockery were this heaven that's
    bending o'er us,
  Glad with the sunshine of the glittering
    May !

But here, where late with naked branches
    striving, —
Wet with the icy tears of wintry grief, —
Across this lonely field of sorrow driving
    The angry tempest whirled the withered
    leaf;

Now swings the pendant bloom, now open-
    ing roses
    Woo the soft zephyrs with their balmy
    breath;
Boughs wave, birds sing, and silver mist
    reposes,
    In bliss, above these emerald waves of
    death.

And sure the Power, that out of desolation
    Can thus the arid wastes of earth relume,
Ne'er meant the crown of all its vast crea-
    tion
    One hour of woe, and then the eternal
    tomb!

But, were this all — were hope with being
    ended,
    In these dark cells that shrine our sacred
    dead;

Were all our prayers and tears in vain ex-
  pended,
  Our passion, labour, faith forever sped ;

Who would not yet — all selfish impulse
  spurning —
  Live for mankind, and triumph with the
  just !
Who, from the field of honour backward
  turning,
  Would trail a sullied ensign in the dust !

Though fate were cruel, human will un-
  daunted,
  Supreme o'er torture, regnant over time,
Can spurn the bitterest foe that ever vaunted
  This mortal frailty which were nature's
  crime !

It may be — every generous trust for-
  bidden —
  That, while these beauteous orbs of ruin
  roll,
From the dark sleep in which the dead are
  hidden
  A flower can wake, but not the human
  soul :

Yet, sweet is every love and every longing;
　Yet shines the dream of heaven in child-
　　hood's eyes;
And troops of angel phantoms still come
　thronging
　To fancy's vision, in the twilight skies:

Yet stirs the heart with nameless, vague
　emotion,
　When moonlight sleeps upon the summer
　　sea;
Yet forest depths and lonely wastes of
　ocean
　And mountain voices set the spirit free:

And, borne on wings of glorious endeavour,
　Man yet can soar above his baser clay —
Throned in high deeds, forever and forever,
　That cannot die, and will not pass away!

II.

High were their deeds, o'er whom our
　hearts are weeping!
　Safe bides their fame, in all men's love
　　and praise!
Hallowed the mould in which their dust is
　sleeping,
　And sweet the memory that has crowned
　　their days!

Ah, once for them young hope unveiled her
    splendour !
Ah, once for them time ran in golden
    sands !
They knew affection's accents, soft and
    tender,
    They felt the touch of loving lips and
        hands.

They saw the awful face of sovereign
    beauty ;
    White arms of proud ambition lured
        them on ;
But in their hearts breathed low the voice
    of duty —
    They heard it, and they answered : they
        are gone.

The midnight wind was cold upon their
    faces, —
    Pale in the silence of the crimson sod ;
But who shall paint through what resplen-
    dent spaces
    Their souls sprang upward to the light
        of God !

No more, for them, in summer twilight's
    glimmer,
    Shall distant music smite the chords of
        pain :

No more, as evening shades grow slowly
    dimmer,
  Shall wandering fragrance pierce the tor-
    tured brain !

No more of lingering doubt, nor stern de-
    nial,
  Nor baffled toil, nor slow, embittering
    strife !
But now, at once, the crown of earthly
    trial, —
  The long, long summer of eternal life !

Calm-fronted, staunch, expectant, and un-
    shaken,
  Who dares the worst that any fate can
    bring —
For him, by iron purpose ne'er forsaken,
  The grave no victory has, and death no
    sting !

We can but serve : some, by the instant
    giving
  Of all that hand could do or heart could
    prize ;
Some, by a meek, laborious, patient living,
  A daily toil, an hourly sacrifice.

We falter on, now hoping, now despairing,
  And hour by hour drag out life's little
    span :
They passed, in one tremendous deed of
    daring, —
  They lived for honour, and they died for
    man !

Pile thick the amaranth and the myrtle o'er
    them —
  For whom our laurelled banners flash and
    flow —
Roses that love and pansies that deplore
    them,
  And lilies, weeping from their hearts of
    snow.

Breathe low, ye murmuring pines, ye whis-
    pering grasses !
  Ye dews of summer night fall softly here !
Be sorrow's sigh in every breeze that
    passes,
  And every rain-drop be a mourner's tear !

And O, ye stars, ye holy lights that cumber
  The deep of heaven, pour benedictions
    down !

N

Shed your sweet incense on this sacred
    slumber —
  Bright as our love, and pure as their re-
    nown !

Breathe our farewell ! ah, very gently
    breathe it, —
  Like ocean's murmur in the coral shell,
And tender as the sea-flowers that en-
    wreathe it, —
  For ever and for evermore, Farewell !

EDWIN BOOTH.

[June 15, 1880.]

I.

His barque will fade, in mist and night,
  Across the dim sea-line,
And coldly on our aching sight
  The solemn stars will shine —
All, all in mournful silence, save
  For ocean's distant roar —
Heard where the slow, regretful wave
  Sobs on the lonely shore.

II.

But, oh, while, winged with love and prayer,
  Our thoughts pursue his track,

What glorious sights the midnight air
  Will proudly waft us back !
What golden words will flutter down
  From many a peak of fame,
What glittering shapes of old renown
  That cluster round his name !

III.

O'er storied Denmark's haunted ground
  Will darkly drift again,
Dream-like and vague, without a sound,
  The spectre of the Dane ;
And breaking hearts will be the wreath
  For grief that knows no tear,
When shine on Cornwall's storm-swept
    heath
  The blazing eyes of Lear.

IV.

Slow, 'mid the portents of the storm
  And fate's avenging powers,
Will moody Richard's haggard form
  Pace through the twilight hours ;
And wildly hurtling o'er the sky
  The red star of Macbeth, —
Torn from the central arch on high, —
  Go down in dusty death !

v.

But — best of all I will softly rise
　His form of manly grace —
The noble brow, the honest eyes,
　The sweetly patient face,
The loving heart, the stately mind
　That, conquering every ill,
Through seas of trouble cast behind,
　Was grandly steadfast still !

VI.

Though skies might gloom and tempest rave,
　Though friends and hopes might fall,
His constant spirit, simply brave,
　Would meet and suffer all —
Would calmly smile at fortune's frown,
　Supreme o'er gain or loss ;
And he the worthiest wears the crown
　That gently bore the cross !

VII.

Be blithe and bright, thou jocund day
　That golden England knows !
Bloom sweetly round the wanderer's way,
　Thou royal English rose !
And English hearts [no need to tell
　How truth itself endures !]

This soul of manhood treasure well,
　Our love commits to yours !

VIII.

Farewell ! nor mist, nor flying cloud,
　Nor night can ever dim
The wreath of honours, pure and proud,
　Our hearts have twined for him !
But bells of memory still shall chime,
　And violets star the sod,
Till our last broken wave of time
　Dies on the shores of God.

ADELAIDE NEILSON.

[Died August 15, 1880.]

And oh, to think the sun can shine,
　The birds can sing, the flowers can bloom,
And she, whose soul was all divine,
　Be darkly mouldering in the tomb :

That o'er her head the night-wind sighs,
　And the sad cypress droops and moans ;
That night has veiled her glorious eyes,
　And silence hushed her heavenly tones :

That those sweet lips no more can smile,
  Nor pity's tender shadows chase,
With many a gentle, child-like wile,
  The rippling laughter o'er her face:

That dust is on the burnished gold
  That floated round her royal head;
That her great heart is dead and cold —
  Her form of fire and beauty dead!

Roll on, gray earth and shining star,
  And coldly mock our dreams of bliss;
There is no glory left to mar,
  Nor any grief so black as this!

———◦◦◦———

JOHN McCULLOUGH.

[APRIL 4, 1881.]

LONG hushed is the harp* that his glory
    had spoken,
  Long stilled is the heart that could sum-
    mon its strain;
Now its chords are all silent, or tuneless,
    or broken,
  What touch can awaken its music again!

* The harp of Moore.

Ah, the breeze in the green dells of Erin is
    blowing !
  If not her great bard yet her spirit can
    flame,
When proud where the waters of Shannon
    are flowing
  Her groves and her temples re-echo his
    name.

Float softly o'er shamrocks, and blue-bells,
    and roses,
  Blend all their gay tints and their odours
    in one ;
And sweet as the zephyr in twilight that
    closes
  Be the kiss of thy love on the brows of
    thy son !

Breathe tenderly o'er us, who cluster
    around him,
  In this, his glad moment of triumph and
    pride :
Deep, deep in our souls are the ties that
    have bound him,
  And life will be lone, with his presence
    denied.

From the arms of the mother, in childhood
    a rover,
  To exile he came, on the wanderer's
    shore :
To the arms of the mother, his trials all
    over,
  And honoured and laurelled, we yield
    him once more.

Speak low of affection that longs to embrace
    him,
  Speak loud of the fame that awaits him
    afar —
When homage shall hail him, and beauty
    shall grace him,
  And pomp hang her wreaths on the con-
    queror's car !

When the shadows of time at his touch
    fall asunder,
  And heroes and demi-gods leap into light ;
When the accents of Brutus ring wild in the
    thunder,
  And the white locks of Lear toss like sea-
    foam in night ;

When the grief of the Moor, like a tempest
    that dashes
  On crags in mid-ocean, has died into rest ;

When the heart of Virginius breaks, o'er
    the ashes
  Of her who was sweetest, and purest, and
    best;

How proudly, how gladly their praise will
    caress him !
  How brightly the jewels will blaze in his
    crown !
How the white hands of honour will greet
    him and bless him
  With lilies and roses of perfect renown !

Ah, grand is the flight of the eagle of morn-
    ing,
  While the dark world beneath him drifts
    into the deep;
But cold as the snow-wreaths the moun-
    tains adorning
  Is the light that illumines his desolate
    sweep.

When the trumpets are blown and the
    standards are streaming,
  And the festal lamps beam on the royal
    array,
How oft will the heart of the monarch be
    dreaming
  Of the home and the friends that are far,
    far away !

There's a pulse in his breast that would
    always regret us —
  It dances in laughter, it trembles in tears ;
With the world at his feet, he would never
    forget us,
  And our hearts would be true, through an
    æon of years !

The cymbals may clash and the gay pennons
    glisten,
  And the clangour of gladness ring jocund
    and free,
But, calm in the tumult, his spirit will listen
  For our whisper of love, floating over the
    sea :

For the music of tones that were once so
    endearing
  (Like a wind of the west o'er a prairie of
    flowers),
But that never again will resound in his
    hearing,
  Except through the tremulous sadness of
    ours.

Ah, manly and tender, thy deeds are thy
    praises !
  Speed on in thy grandeur, all peerless and
    lone,

And greet, in old England, her hawthorns
    and daisies, —
  A spirit as gentle and bright as their own !

Speed on, wheresoever fame's angel may
    guide thee !
  No fancy can dream and no language can
    tell
What faith and what blessings walk ever
    beside thee,
  Or the depth of our love as we bid thee
    Farewell.

LAWRENCE BARRETT.

[JUNE 7, 1881.]

I.

WHEN from his gaze our shores receding
  In night and distance drift away,
And, every present joy unheeding,
  He turns to muse, and grieve, and pray,
How will regret and memory, meeting,
  This brilliant scene bring back to view,
And hear once more your manly greeting,
  And sigh once more his fond adieu !

II.

And we, by sadness made more tender,
  As here we knit our broken chain —
How gladly will affection render
  Our gentle tribute once again !
How sweet 'twill be, though joys are
        thwarted,
  And smiles rebuked by sorrow's sigh,
To think, however friends are parted,
  At least that friendship cannot die !

III.

His eyes will look on English meadows
  Where scarlet poppies smile and dream ;
And he will muse where wandering shadows
  Drift over Avon's sacred stream ;
And, mind and soul in bondage taken,
  Will roam those temples strange and vast
Where every pensive step will waken
  The glorious memories of the past.

IV.

But we shall hear, in grief beclouded,
  Poor Harebell mourn his ruined home ;
And see, in night and tempest shrouded,
  Grim Cassius pace the stones of Rome ;

With grizzled Yorick, frenzy-ridden,
 From passion's fevered dream awake ;
And feel, with tears that flow unbidden,
 The royal heart of Scotland break.

v.

O, art divine, supreme, undying —
 Not time nor space can e'er subdue !
The seas roll on — the years are flying —
 Man passes — thou alone art true !
No cloud can dim their deathless lustre
 Whose names thy angel hands enroll,
Nor blight the shining shapes that cluster
 In thy pantheon of the soul !

vi.

Yet, many a cherished tie is broken,
 Across that darkening waste of sea ! —
They make no sign, they send no token,
 They come not back to love and me.
I know where, deaf to blames and praises,
 In youth and beauty cold and dead,
Rests now beneath old England's daisies
 Her tenderest heart, her loveliest head !

vii.

And him we cast the roses after
 Whose cynic smile was humour's kiss —

Whose magic turned the world to laugh-
    ter —
  Where dwells he, in an hour like this ? . . .
Ah, let us think, though gone before us, —
  The vanished friends of days no more, —
They watch with fond affection o'er us,
  And bless us, from their heavenly shore.

VIII.

I see the radiant phantoms thronging,
  To clasp him in their guardian thrall !
I bless him, by each noble longing
  That e'er his gentle lips let fall !
By all high thought and pure devotion —
  By towering pine and nestling rose !
Farewell, farewell ! on land or ocean —
  God bless him, wheresoe'er he goes !

A MEMORY.

[G. A. — October, 1881.]

I.

The peace of this autumnal day
Allures my dreaming thoughts away
To that great world beyond the deep,
Where I so many treasures keep.

There, fond and true, one friend I find,
Whose tender heart and constant mind
Gave, while he lingered here on earth,
Comfort, and cheer, and hope, and mirth ;
And still they waft a cordial breath
Across the icy waves of death.
His nature, while he dwelt below,
Was like these days : this season's glow,
The misty sky, the sleeping sea,
The browning grass, the burnished tree,
The wild-flowers, swinging o'er the brook,
Were in his heart as in his book.
Alive, he charmed away life's fret
With all the sunshine he could get,
And, when death whispered, softly crept
Into a quiet place and slept ;
And nature never saw such grace
As hallowed then his noble face.
And so, to think upon him here,
In this sweet season of the year, —
Which he so loved, which he was like
As clouds are to the clouds they strike, —
Is winning peace, and strength to live,
Beyond what all the world can give.

II.

Ah, not to me, dear heart, was said
The word that crowned thy royal head

First with the aureole's light and bloom,
And then the amaranth of the tomb.
Fate gave thee power, and calm, and poise,
And all thy days and deeds were joys.
Thine were the forest and the flood,
The sunrise sparkled in thy blood,
And thou didst hold a careless flight
Above the dells and caves of night.
But ever through thy smile shone clear
The lustre of compassion's tear,
The pity of thy gentle mind,
And tenderness, for all mankind.
I saw thee with a wistful eye,
And saddened — and I knew not why;
Till soon, too soon, thy summons came,
And thou wert nothing but a name.
Ah, day of misery and of moan,
When grief and I were left alone !

III.

Fate gave not me her smile benign —
That pensive, playful calm of thine —
But early from her bosom cast,
To be the sport of every blast,
To war with passion, and to know
The sting of want, the pang of woe, —
Forcing a soul, for kindness born,
To every strife it held in scorn.

So, careless whether right or wrong,
I battled through the hostile throng,
And felt, whatever doom might be,
Or life or death, the same to me.
'Twas then across my pathway lone
The holy star of friendship shone!
'Twas then thy kindness soothed my pain,
And arched the heaven of hope again!
As, sudden through the stormy dark,
Full on the tempest-battered barque,
Home's glad and golden beacons shine,
So flashed thy spirit upon mine:
And not, though hope's last star were set
Could this true heart of mine forget!

IV.

Now, of our few but happy years
Remains this flower, that bloomed in tears:
  Not of the crown of life bereft
  Is he who yet has patience left.
The haggard sky, the surf's dull roar,
The midnight storm, are mine no more:
But mine the gleam of setting sun,
The call of birds when day is done,
The last, sad light, so loath to pass
It weeps upon the golden grass,
The sigh of leaves, in evening air,
The distant bell that calls to prayer, —

o

And nothing from my spirit bars
The benediction of the stars.

v.

Ah, loved so well and mourned so long,
Here in my heart as in my song,
To thy dear memory let me raise
One tender strain of other days,
One pæan to the good thou wast,
One low lament for all I lost.
Yet, looking o'er life's arid track,
Kind soul, I would not wish thee back.
What sadder lot, what doom of fate,
More sterile is, more desolate,
Than here to goad our wearied powers,
And toil through times that are not ours!
Ah, no, the silence now is best,
The leaf down-fluttering o'er thy rest,
And every kind, caressing sigh
That nature breathes o'er those that die;
While thou, in some serener sphere,
Forgett'st the toils and troubles here;
Or, made a part of flowers and trees,
Art pure, and calm, and safe, like these.
—Slow pales the light; the day declines;
The night-wind murmurs in the pines;
The stars come out, and, far away,
Across the sweetly sleeping bay

One snow-white sail, by sunset kist,
Fades slowly in the ocean mist,
Fades — like all joys and griefs we know,
And like this dream of Long Ago.

LONGFELLOW.

[DIED MARCH 24, 1882.]

ALONE, at night, he heard them sigh —
  These wild March winds that beat his
     tomb —
Alone, at night, from those that die,
  He sought one ray to light his gloom.

And still he heard the night-winds moan,
  And still the mystery closed him round,
And still the darkness, cold and lone,
  Sent forth no ray, returned no sound.

But time at last the answer brings,
  And he, past all our suns and snows,
At rest with peasants and with kings,
  Like them the wondrous secret knows.

Alone, at night, we hear them sigh —
  These wild March winds that stir his
     pall ;

And, helpless, wandering, lost, we cry
  To his dim ghost to tell us all.

He loved us while he lingered here ;
  We loved him — never love more true !
He will not leave in doubt and fear
  The human grief that once he knew.

For never yet was born the day
  When, faint of heart and weak of limb,
One suffering creature turned away,
  Unhelped, unsoothed, uncheered by him !

But still through darkness, dense and
    bleak,
  The winds of March moan wildly round,
And still we feel that all we seek
  Ends in that sigh of vacant sound.

He cannot tell us — none can tell
  What waits behind the mystic veil !
Yet he who lived and died so well,
  In that, perchance, has told the tale.

Not to the wastes of nature drift —
  Else were this world an evil dream —
The crown and soul of nature's gift,
  By Avon or by Charles's stream !

His song was like the pine-tree's sigh,
  At midnight o'er a poet's grave,
Or like the sea-bird's distant cry,
  Borne far across the twilight wave.

There is no flower of meek delight,
  There is no star of heavenly pride,
That shines not fairer and more bright
  Because he lived, loved, sang, and died.

Wild winds of March, his requiem sing !
  Weep o'er him, April's sorrowing skies !
Till come the tender buds of spring
  To deck the pillow where he lies :

Till violets pour their purple flood,
  That wandering myrtle shall not lack,
And, royal with the summer's blood,
  The roses that he loved come back :

Till all that nature gives of light,
  To rift the gloom and point the way,
Shall sweetly pierce our mortal night,
  And symbol his immortal day !

WILLIAM WARREN.[5]

RED globes of autumn strew the sod,
    The bannered woods wear crimson
        shields,
The aster and the golden-rod
    Deck all the fields.

No clarion blast, at morning blown,
    Should greet the way-worn veteran here,
Nor roll of drum nor trumpet-tone
    Assail his ear.

No jewelled ensigns now should smite,
    With jarring flash, down emerald steeps,
Where sweetly in the sunset light
    The valley sleeps.

No bolder ray should bathe this bower
    Than when, above the glimmering stream,
The crescent moon, in twilight's hour,
    First sheds her beam.

No ruder note should break the thrall,
    That love and peace and honour weave,
Than some lone wild-bird's gentle call,
    At summer eve.

But here should float the voice of song —
　Like evening winds in autumn leaves,
Sweet with the balm they waft along
　　From golden sheaves.

The sacred past should feel its spell,
　And here should murmur, soft and low,
The voices that he loved so well, —
　　Long, long ago.

The vanished scenes should give to this
　The cherished forms of other days,
And rosy lips that felt his kiss
　　Breathe out his praise.

The comrades of his young renown
　Should proudly throng around him now,
When falls the spotless laurel crown
　　Upon his brow.

Not in their clamorous shouts who make
　The noonday pomp of glory's lord
Does the true soul of manhood take
　　Its high reward.

But when from all the glimmering years
　Beneath the moonlight of the past
The strong and tender spirit hears
　　' Well done,' at last ;

When love looks forth from heavenly eyes,
 And heavenly voices make acclaim,
And all his deeds of kindness rise
 To bless his name;

When all that has been sweetly blends
 With all that is, and both revere
The life so lovely in its ends,
 So pure, so dear;

Then leaps indeed the golden flame
 Of blissful pride to rapture's brim —
The fire that sacramental fame
 Has lit for him!

For him who, lord of joy and woe,
 Through half a century's snow-white
 years
Has gently ruled, in humour's glow,
 The fount of tears.

True, simple, earnest, patient, kind,
 Through griefs that many a weaker will
Had stricken dead, his noble mind
 Was constant still.

Sweet, tender, playful, thoughtful, droll,
 His gentle genius still has made

Mirth's perfect sunshine in the soul,
    And pity's shade.

With amaranths of eternal spring
    Be all his life's calm evening drest,
While summer winds around him sing
    The songs of rest !

And thou, O Memory, strange and dread,
    That stand'st on heaven's ascending
        slope,
Lay softly on his reverend head
    The wreath of hope !

So softly, — when the port he wins,
    To which life's happiest breezes blow, —
That where earth ends and heaven begins
    He shall not know.

———◦———

GOOD-NIGHT.

[W. A. S. — DIED JANUARY 7, 1883.]

' GOOD-NIGHT, my boy '; and with a smile
    He turned his steps and sped away :
Since then 'tis but a little while,
    And he is dead to-day :

Dead — and the friend that once I knew,
  My comrade both in joy and pain,
So often tried and always true,
  Will never smile again.

His days were many, and the world
  Had most of all his thought and care ;
But now his sails of toil were furled
  In art's serener air.
The evening lamp, the storied page,
  The mantling glass, the song, the jest —
These turned the twilight of his age
  To morning and to rest.

The thorny paths of life he knew ;
  His tender heart was quick to feel ;
And wounds his pity wept to view,
  His bounty glowed to heal.
Of worldly ways, of frailty's slips,
  Of mortal sin, he had his share ;
Yet still could breathe, with childhood's lips,
  His artless childhood's prayer.

Good deeds were all the work he wrought;
  Sweet thoughts and merry all he prized;
Nor power nor fame by him was sought,
  Nor homely life despised.

Strife could not live before his face,
    But wheresoe'er his footsteps fell
Came kindness, with its smile of grace,
    And everything was well.

He did not strive to win the heights;
    Enough for him the lowly vale,
The autumn sunset's pensive lights,
    The autumn's perfumed gale :
But toilers on the upward slope,
    Who greatly strove and bravely dared,
Had cheer of him, and felt new hope,
    Howe'er their fortune fared.

To brighten life, where'er he went,
    With laughter's sparkle, and to make
Home's fireside lovely with content,
    For gentle humour's sake —
That was his fate.   Ah, darkly shows
    The path where yesterday he shone, —
That downward path of many woes
    That we must tread, alone.

Yet he, like us, had lost and grieved :
    He knew how hard it is to bear,
When, lone and listless and bereaved,
    We sink in dumb despair :

And could those lips, now marble chill,
  But speak once more from that true heart,
With what a jocund, blithe good-will
  They'd bid our grief depart !

It was but yesterday he went :
  This is the room and that the door :
When some few idle days are spent
  'Twill all be as before :
The heavenly morning will destroy
  This rueful dream of death and pain,
And I shall hear him say, ' My boy,'
  And clasp his hand again.

HENRY IRVING.

I.—AVE. November 18, 1883.

If we could win from Shakespeare's river
  The music of its murmuring flow,
With all the wild-bird notes that quiver
  Where Avon's scarlet meadows glow ;
If we could twine with joy at meeting
  Their prayers who lately grieved to part,
Ah, then indeed our song of greeting
  Might find an echo in his heart !

But though we cannot, in our singing,
   That music and those prayers entwine,
At least we'll set our blue-bells ringing
   And he shall hear our whispering pine;
And these shall breathe a welcome royal,
   In accents tender, sweet, and kind,
From lips as fond and hearts as loyal
   As any that he left behind.

II.—VALE. APRIL 29, 1884.

Far off beyond the shining sea,
   Where scarlet poppies glisten,
And daisies on the emerald lea
   Lift up their heads and listen,
Where Thames and Avon glance and glow,
   To-day the waters, straying,
Will murmur in their tranquil flow
   The words that we are saying.

Ah, not in parting hours alone
   Is fond affection spoken:
The love that weeps in sorrow's moan
   Still smiles in welcome's token.
Farewell, farewell our hearts will sigh,
   When void and dark his place is;
But 'Well for me' is England's cry,
   To him her love embraces!

Farewell, thou child of many a prayer!
   While lonely we deplore thee,
All crystal be the seas that bear
   And skies that sparkle o'er thee.
Thy mother's heart, thy mother's lip
   Will soon once more caress thee—
We can but watch thy lessening ship
   And, in our silence, bless thee!

But let the golden waves leap up
   While yet our hearts beat near him!
No bitter drop be in the cup
   With which our hope would cheer him!
Pour the red roses at his feet!
   Wave laurel boughs above him!
And if we part or if we meet
   Be glad and proud to love him!

His life has made this iron age
   More grand and fair in story;
Illumed our Shakespeare's sacred page
   With new and deathless glory;
Refreshed the love of noble fame
   In hearts all sadly faring,
And lit anew the dying flame
   Of genius and of daring.

Long may his radiant summer smile
   Where Albion's rose is dreaming,

And over art's Hesperian isle
  His royal banner streaming ;
While every trumpet blast that rolls
  From Britain's lips to hail him
Is echoed in our kindred souls,
  Whose truth can never fail him.

On your white wings, ye angel years,
  Through roseate sunshine springing,
Waft fortune from all happier spheres,
  With garlands and with singing ;
Make strong that tender heart and true —
  That thought of heaven to guide him —
And blessings pour, like diamond dew,
  On her that walks beside him !

And when is said the last farewell,
  So solemn and so certain,
And fate shall strike the prompter's bell,
  To drop the final curtain,
Be his, whom every muse hath blest,
  That best of earthly closes —
To sink to rest on England's breast,
  And sleep beneath her roses.

III. — VALE. APRIL 6, 1885.

Now fades across the glimmering deep, now
    darkly drifts away
The royal monarch of our hearts, the glory
    of our day ;

The pale stars shine, the night wind sighs,
    the sad sea makes its moan,
And we, bereft, are standing here, in silence
    and alone.

Gone every shape of power and dread his
    magic touch could paint;
Gone haunted Aram's spectral face, and
    England's martyred saint;
Gone Mathias, of the frenzied soul, and
    Louis' sceptred guile,
The gentle head of poor Lesurques, and
    Hamlet's holy smile.

No more in gray Messina's halls shall love
    and revel twine;
No more on Portia's midnight bowers the
    moon of summer shine;
No golden barge on Hampton's stream
    salute the perfumed shore;
No ghost on Denmark's rampart cliff af-
    fright our pulses more!

The morning star of art, he rose across the
    eastern sea
To wake the slumbering harp and set the
    frozen fountain free;

Now, wrapt in glory's mist, he seeks his
    orient skies again ;
And tender thoughts in sorrowing hearts
    are all that must remain. . . .

Slow fade, across a drearier sea, beneath a
    darker sky,
The dreams that cheer, the lights that lure,
    the baffled hopes that die :
Youth's trust, love's bliss, ambition's pride
    — the white wings all are flown,
And memory walks the lonely shore, indif-
    ferent and alone.

Yet sometimes o'er that shadowy deep, by
    wandering breezes blown,
Float odours from Hesperian isles, with
    music's organ tone,
And something stirs within the breast, a
    secret, nameless thrill,
To say, though worn and sear and sad, our
    hearts are human still ; —

If not the torrid diamond wave that made
    young life sublime,
If not the tropic rose that bloomed in every
    track of time,

P

If not exultant passion's glow, when all
 the world was fair,
At least one flash of heaven, one breath of
 art's immortal air !

Ah, God, make bright, for many a year, on
 Beauty's heavenly shrine,
This hallowed fire that Thou hast lit, this
 sacred soul of Thine !
While love's sweet light and sorrow's tear, —
 life's sunshine dimmed with showers —
Shall keep for aye his memory green in
 these true hearts of ours !

ELEGY AT EVERGREEN.[6]

[ELEGY SPOKEN AT THE DEDICATION OF THE ACTORS'
 MONUMENT IN EVERGREEN CEMETERY, BROOKLYN,
 N.Y., JUNE 6, 1887.]

I.

COULD we but feel that our lost ones are
 near us —
 We in our darkness and they in their
 light —

Could we but feel that they see us and hear
 us,
 Ah, what a splendour would stream
 through the night !
How this great world, in its jubilant
 madness,
 Hopeless no longer, nor vagrant, nor
 blind,
Grandly would blaze through the heaven of
 gladness,
 Spurning the cloud of its sorrow behind !

II.

Still soars the jest to the echoing rafter,
 Still the gay throng sparkles over the
 scene,
Still the sweet air is a ripple of laughter,
 Red gleams the rose and the myrtle is
 green ;
Still the lights flash and the trumpet is
 sounding,
 Pennons are fluttered and banners un-
 furled —
Where is the grace and the genius abound-
 ing
 Once that redeemed and illumined the
 world ?

III.

Where are the hearts that were tenderly
plighted,
Long years ago, in the kingdom of flowers?
Where are the hands that were fondly
united?
Where are the eyes that looked love into
ours?
Yesterday was it, that vainly we hearkened,
Hearing no longer the one cherished
tone?
Yesterday was it, the heavens were
darkened,
Leaving us stricken, bewildered, and
lone?

IV.

Little by little the roof-tree is crumbled,
Slow from the branches the leaves drop
away,
Year after year we are broken and humbled,
Nearing the desolate end of the play.
Red in the west, where the cloud-rack is
scattered,
Lowers, defeated, the fugitive sun;
Dreary and cold, like the life it has shat-
tered,
Night covers all and our journey is done.

V.

Is there no more, when this pageant is
    ended ? . . .
  Here, where they slumber, the violet
    blows ;
Here with the bird-note divinely are blended
  Soul of the lily and heart of the rose !
What though the rage of the tempest may
    cover,
  White with its anger, the shuddering
    plain —
Soon will the kiss of its heavenly lover
  Thrill it to verdure and beauty again.

VI.

Ah, when we burst from this fettered
    existence,
  Born into freedom and loosed into space,
How shall we spurn, at what infinite dis-
    tance,
  All that has bound us in earthly disgrace !
Who shall conceive what the soul may
    inherit !
  Who shall declare the unspeakable bliss
Regnant and safe, in that world, for the
    spirit
  True to the right, through the trials of
    this !

VII.

Dark for them, now, whom we hallow and
    honour,
    Dark and forlorn is the stage that was
      theirs ;
Peace, with the garment of silence upon her,
    Broods o'er the dust of their sorrows and
      cares.
Low lie their heads with the clods of the
    valley ;
    Never again will they come at our call ;
Vainly around their cold ashes we rally ;
    Quenched are the lights, and the curtain
      must fall.

VIII.

Ends not this world in the night of denial !
    Not for a grave were illumined the
      spheres !
Forward and far from this bondage and
    trial
    Love reaps, in rapture, the harvest of tears.
Only for us is the pang of bereavement ;
    Theirs the same mission, yet more than
      the same —
Loftier powers, and nobler achievement
    Wrought with the music of sweeter
      acclaim !

IX.

Labour and pain, that were never requited,
  Passionate hope, that was never fulfilled,
Dreams and desires, that were baffled and
    blighted,
  Pure aspirations, defeated and chilled,
Weary vicissitude, strife, and dejection, —
  Fate gave them these, till it gave them
    release :
Here the great heart of a comrade affection
  Gathers them home to the bosom of peace.

X.

Hallowed be ever this dream-haunted haven:
  Hallowed the shaft that we consecrate
    here !
Never may ominous pinion of raven
  Herald the spectre oblivion near !
Sentinel roses, bloom faithful and tender !
  Guardian heavens, smile lovingly down, —
Clouds in your sorrow and stars in your
    splendour, —
  Pouring the incense of deathless renown !

XI.

Echoes of blessing, — from where, in our
    vision,
  Hearts never falter and eyes never
    weep, —

Blown on wild winds from the mountains
    elysian,
Drift, in sweet requiems, over their sleep !
Lift up our souls — till with pæans and
    dirges
Merciful death shall at last set us free —
There, where the moan of the infinite
    surges
Dies on the shore of eternity's sea !

———◦◦◦———

RAYMOND.⁷

[An Epitaph.]

His restless spirit, while on earth he dwelt,
Wreathed with a smile whatever grief he
    felt, —
And 'twas his lot, though crowned with
    public praise,
Ample and warm, to walk in troubled ways.
Glad was his voice, that all men laughed to
    hear,
While few surmised the pang, the secret
    tear.
Yet did that thrill of pathos flush the
    grace
Of playful humour in his speaking face,

Inform his fancy and inspire his art
To cheer the senses and to touch the heart.
Jocund and droll, incessant, buoyant,
    quaint,
His vigour fired the forms his skill could
    paint,
Till, over-anxious lest effects were tame,
He left his picture, to adorn its frame.
A mind more serious never did engage
Through simulated mirth the comic stage,
Nor strong ambition conquer and control
A sturdier will and more aspiring soul.
If haply, much constrained, his purpose
    bowed
To woo the fancy of the fickle crowd,
Yet did his judgment spurn the poor re-
    nown
Of shallow jester and of trivial clown.
A true comedian this, by fate designed
To picture manners and to cheer mankind.
So RAYMOND lived — and naught remains to
    tell,
Save that too soon the final curtain fell.
Peace to his dust, where love and honour
    weep,
In endless sorrow, o'er their comrade's
    sleep.

1887.

LESTER WALLACK.[8]

[DECEMBER 17, 1887.]

I.

WITH a glimmer of plumes and a sparkle of
       lances,
    With blare of the trumpet and neigh of
       the steed,
At morning they rode where the bright river
       glances
    And the sweet summer wind ripples over
       the mead.
The green sod beneath them was ermined
       with daisies,
    Smiling up to green boughs tossing wild
       in their glee,
While a thousand glad hearts sang their
       honours and praises,
    Where the knights of the mountain rode
       down to the sea.

II.

One rode 'neath the banner whose face was
       the fairest,
    Made royal with deeds that his manhood
       had done,

And the halo of blessing fell richest and
    rarest
  On his armour that splintered the shafts
    of the sun. —
So moves o'er the waters the cygnet se-
    dately ;
  So waits the strong eagle to mount on the
    wing ;
Serene and puissant and simple and stately,
  So shines among princes the form of the
    king ! . . .

III.

With a gay bugle-note, when the daylight's
    last glimmer
  Smites, crimson and gold, on the snow of
    his crest,
At evening he rides, through the shades
    growing dimmer,
  While the banners of sunset stream red
    in the west.
His comrades of morning are scattered and
    parted —
  The clouds hanging low and the winds
    making moan —
But, smiling and dauntless and calm and
    true-hearted,
  All proudly he rides down the valley,
    alone.

IV.

Sweet gales of the woodland, embrace and
  caress him !
  White wings of renown, be his comfort
  and light !
Pale dews of the star-beam, encompass and
  bless him
  With the peace and the balm and the
  glory of night !
And, oh, while he wends to the verge of
  that ocean
  Where the years, like a garland, shall fall
  from his brow,
May his glad heart exult in the tender devotion —
  The love that encircles and hallows him
  now !

THE STATUE.

[Spoken at the Dedication of a Monument to
  the Tragedian John McCullough, in Mount
  Moriah Cemetery, Philadelphia, November 28,
  1888.]

I.

How different now, old friend, the meeting !
  Thy form, thy face, thy look the same —

But where is now the kindly greeting,
  The voice of cheer, the heart of flame ?
There, in thy grandeur, calm and splen-
    did, —
God's peace on that imperial brow, —
Thou standest, grief and trouble ended,
  And we are nothing to thee now.

II.

Yet once again the air is cloven
  With joyous tumult of acclaim ;
Once more the golden wreaths are woven,
  Of love and honour, for thy name ;
And round thee here, with tender longing,
  As oft they did in days of old,
The comrades of thy soul come thronging,
  Who never knew thee stern or cold.

III.

Why waits, in frozen silence sleeping,
  The smile that made our hearts rejoice ?
Why, dead to laughing and to weeping,
  Is hushed the music of thy voice ?
By what strange mood of reverie haunted
  Art thou, the gentle, grown austere ?
And do we live in dreams enchanted,
  To know thee gone, yet think thee here ?

IV.

Ah, fond pretence ! ah, sweet beguiling !
   Too well I know thy course is run.
There's no more grief and no more smiling
   For thee henceforth beneath the sun.
In manhood's noon thy summons found thee,
   In glory's blaze, on fortune's height,
Trailed the black robe of doom around thee,
   And veiled thy radiant face in night.

V.

This but the shadow of a vision
   Our mourning souls alone can see,
That pierce through death to realms elysian
   More hallowed now because of thee.
Yet, oh, what heart, with recollection
   Of thy colossal trance of pain,
Were now so selfish in affection
   To wish thee back from heaven again !

VI.

There must be, in those boundless spaces
   Where thy great spirit wanders free,
Abodes of bliss, enchanted places,
   That only love's white angels see !
And sure, if heavenly kindness showered
   On every sufferer 'neath the sun

Shows any human spirit dowered
  With love angelic, thou wert one !

VII.

There's no grand impulse, no revealing,
  In all the glorious world of art,
There's no sweet thought or noble feeling
  That throbbed not in thy manly heart !
There's no strong flight of aspiration,
  No reverent dream of realms divine,
No pulse, no thrill, no proud elation
  Of god-like power that was not thine !

VIII.

So stand forever, joyless, painless,
  Supreme alike o'er smiles and tears,
Thou true man's image, strong and stain-
    less,
  Unchanged through all the changing
    years —
While fame's blue crystal o'er thee bending
  With honour's gems shall blaze and burn,
And rose and lily, round thee blending,
  Adorn and bless thy hallowed urn !

IX.

While summer days are long and lonely,
  While autumn sunshine seems to weep,

While midnight hours are bleak, and only
　The stars and clouds their vigils keep,
All gentle things that live shall moan thee,
　All fond regrets forever wake ;
For earth is happier having known thee,
　And heaven is sweeter for thy sake !

WHITELAW REID.

I. — Honour's Pearl.

[May 3, 1889.]

I.

Because in danger's darkest hour,
　When heart and hope sank low,
She nerved our frail and faltering power
　To brave its mightiest foe ;
Because our fathers smiled to see
　Her golden lilies dance
O'er the proud field that made us free,
　We plight our faith to France !

II.

Ah, grand and sweet the holy bond,
　That who gives all is blest !

And love can give no pledge beyond
  The life she loves the best.
That pledge these hallowed rites declare,
  Of choice and not of chance —
And he shall cross the sea to bear
  Our loyal hearts to France !

III.

Strong, tender, gentle, patient, wise,
  Brave soul and constant mind,
True wit, that kindles as it flies
  And leaves no grief behind, —
Be thine to wear the snowy plume
  And poise the burnished lance —
Our rose of chivalry, to bloom
  Among the knights of France !

IV.

Be thine the glorious task to speed
  The conquering age of gold —
Till ravaged peace no more shall bleed,
  Till history's muse behold
Borne in the vanward, fast and far,
  Of the free world's advance,
Blent with Columbia's bannered star,
  The triple stripes of France !

Q

242WANDERERS.

II. — Thure et Fidibus.

[April 30, 1892.]

I.

Dark streamers of the eastern gale,
  Blown far across the desert sea,
Your wings have filled the snowy sail,
  That bears my comrade back to me !
Through glist'ning surge and flying foam,
Your stormy pinions waft him home.

II.

Cold waves that beat the murmuring
    shore, —
  Sad pulsing throbs of ocean's breast, —
Your grieving cadence mourns no more,
  Your sobbing requiem dies to rest, —
When now, by all fame's banners fanned,
The laurelled wanderer comes to land.

III.

No longer now our weary eyes
  Gaze down the empty ocean track :
No more we muse, with stifled sighs,
  On ships that sailed and came not back, —
Glad hopes that flew, on fancy's wing,
When all the world was love and spring.

IV.

For now the hollow cave of night,
   The silent deep of time and space,
Through many a rift of diamond light,
   Yields up our argosy of grace ;
And all sweet airs of heaven enfold
Its silver sails and spars of gold.

V.

The lion heart that never quailed,
   The patient spirit, sweetly wise,
The equal mind, howe'er assailed
   By grief that blights and time that tries —
Those are the glories that she bore,
And those the riches come to shore.

VI.

There should be fairer flowers than these,
   And all the bells of joy should fling
Their music on the perfumed breeze,
   With sweeter songs than I can sing —
On whose frail harp the sunset ray
Of passion long has died away.

VII.

Yet once again its fragile strings,
   Slow trembling to my trembling touch,

Shall softly wake to hallow things
  So precious and beloved so much —
Truth, valour, kindness — all that blend
To make the champion and the friend !

VIII.

His world of hope be crowned in this !
  Bloom round him, wheresoe'er he goes,
White lilies of perpetual bliss,
  Entwined with honour's fadeless rose !
May all be his that love can give
And all for which 'tis life to live !

A SACRIFICE.

[D. D. L. — Died September 5, 1889.]

Early, but not too early for thy fame,
  The seal of silence on thy lips is laid,
While we, aghast, disheartened, and dis-
      mayed,
    Crush back our tears and softly speak
      thy name.
    To us it has one meaning and the same —
A brave and gentle soul, a noble mind,
Pure, constant, generous, modest and re-
      fined,

With simple duty for its only aim.
Dear are the days that thou hast left be-
    hind,
  By sweet words hallowed, and by kindly
    deeds ;
  And thus the heart of sorrow moans and
    bleeds,
And ever bleeds, and will not be resigned —
  Knowing its hopeless hope is all in vain,
  To see thy face or hear thy voice again.

WILKIE COLLINS.

[DIED SEPTEMBER 23, 1889.]

I.

OFTEN and often, when the days were
    dark
  And, whether to remember or behold,
  Life was a burden, and my heart, grown
    old
With sorrow, scarce was conscious, did I
    mark
  How from thy distant place across the
    sea,
  Vibrant with hope and with emotion free

Thy voice of cheer rose like the morning
    lark —
And that was comfort if not joy to me !
For in the weakness of our human grief
    The mind that does not break and will
      not bend
Teaches endurance as the one true friend,
The steadfast anchor and the sure relief.
    That was thy word, and what thy precept
      taught
    Thy life made regnant in one living
      thought.

II.

Thy vision saw the halo of romance
    Round every common thing that men
      behold.
    Thy lucid art could turn to precious
      gold, —
Like roseate motes that in the sunbeams
    dance, —
Whatever object met thy kindling glance ;
    And in that mirror life was never cold.
A gracious warmth suffused thy sparkling
    page,
    And woman's passionate heart by thee
      was drawn,
    With all the glorious colours of the dawn,

Against the background of this pagan age —
Her need of love, her sacrifice, her trance
  Of patient pain, her weary pilgrimage!
Thou knewest all of grief that can be
    known,
And didst portray all sorrows but thine
    own.

III.

Where shall I turn, now that thy lips are
    dumb
  And night is on those eyes that loved me
    well?
  What other voice, across thy dying
    knell,
With like triumphant notes of power will
    come?
Alas! my ravaged heart is still and numb
  With thinking of the blank that must
    remain!
  Yet be it mine, amid these wastes of
    pain,
Where all must falter and where many
    sink,
To stay the foot of misery on the brink
  Of dark despair, to bid blind sorrow
    see —
  Teaching that human will breaks every
    chain

When once endurance sets the spirit
    free ;
And, living thus thy perfect faith, to think
I am to others what thou wert to me !

Steamship *Aurania*, Mid-ocean, October 10, 1889.

———•◦•———

MISERIMUS.

[C. W. T. — DIED APRIL 12, 1891.]

I.

FREED from the strife of this world and the
    scorn of it,
  Sweetly he sleeps on the emerald plain !
Never ambition, nor sorrow that's born of
    it —
  Sceptre or cross — can afflict him again !
All that he lived for was truth and the fight
    for it ;
  Now all his battles are over and done.
Death gives him slumber, at last, and the
    night for it —
  Trials all ended and victory won !

II.

They that reviled him may mourn to re-
    cover him —
  Knowing how gentle he was and how
    brave !

Nothing he'll reck, where the wind blowing
    over him
    Ripples the grasses that dream on his
      grave !
Though to our vision this dust be the last
    of him,
    Low in the ground and deserted and lone,
Time will avenge all the woe that is past of
    him,
    Fate will remember and justice atone.

III.

After the fray and the heart-breaking pain
    of it,
    Aliened affection and honour betrayed,
Here is the end and the crown and the gain
    of it —
    Cold in the earth where the victor is
      laid.
Stars will watch over him, silence lament
    for him,
    Soft woodland whispers re-echo his
      knell —
Bird-note and leaf-murmur tenderly blent
    for him —
    Comrade and brother and friend, Fare
      thee well !

FLORENCE.

[An Epitaph.]

By Virtue cherished, by Affection mourned,
By Honour hallowed, and by Fame adorned,
Here FLORENCE sleeps, and o'er his sacred
    rest
Each word is tender and each thought is
    blest.
Long, for his loss, shall pensive Mem'ry
    show
Through Humour's mask, the visage of her
    woe,
Day breathe a darkness that no sun dispels,
And Night be full of whispers and farewells;
While patient Kindness, shadow-like and
    dim,
Droops in its loneliness, bereft of him,
Feels its sad doom and sure decadence
    nigh, —
For how should Kindness live, when he
    could die!

The eager heart, that felt for every grief,
The bounteous hand, that loved to give
    relief,

The honest smile, that blessed where'er it
    lit,
The dew of pathos and the sheen of wit,
The sweet blue eyes, the voice of melting
    tone
That made all hearts as gentle as his own ;
The Actor's charm, supreme in royal thrall,
That ranged through every field and shone
    in all —
For these must Sorrow make perpetual
    moan,
Bereaved, benighted, hopeless, and alone ?
Ah, no : for Nature does no act amiss,
And heaven were lonely but for souls like
    this.

GEORGE WILLIAM CURTIS.

[DIED AUGUST 31, 1892.]

I.

ALL the flowers were in their pride
On the day when Rupert died.

Dreamily, through dozing trees,
Sighed the idle summer breeze.

Wild birds, glancing in the air,
Spilled their music everywhere.

Not one sign of mortal ill
Told that his great heart was still.

Now the grass he loved to tread
Murmurs softly o'er his head:

Now the great green branches wave
High above his lonely grave:

While, in grief's perpetual speech,
Roll the breakers on the beach.

Oh, my comrade, oh, my friend,
Must this parting be the end?

II.

Weave the shroud and spread the pall!
Night and silence cover all.

Howsoever we deplore,
They who go return no more.

Never from that unknown track
Floats one answering whisper back.

Nature, vacant, will not heed
Lips that grieve or hearts that bleed.

Wherefore now should mourning word
Or the tearful dirge be heard?

How shall words our grief abate? —
Call him noble; call him great;

Say that faith, now gaunt and grim,
Once was fair because of him;

Say that goodness, round his way,
Made one everlasting day;

Say that beauty's heavenly flame
Bourgeoned wheresoe'er he came;

Say that all life's common ways
Were made glorious in his gaze;

Say he gave us, hour by hour,
Hope and patience, grace and power;

Say his spirit was so true
That it made us noble too; —

What is this, but to declare
Life's bereavement, Love's despair?

What is this, but just to say
All we loved is torn away?

Weave the shroud and spread the pall!
Night and silence cover all.

III.

Oh, my comrade, oh, my friend,
Must this parting be the end?

Heart and hope are growing old :
Dark the night comes down, and cold :

Few the souls that answer mine,
And no voice so sweet as thine.

Desert wastes of care remain —
Yet thy lips speak not again !

Gray eternities of space —
Yet nowhere thy living face !

Only now the lonesome blight,
Heavy day and haunted night.

All the light and music reft —
Only thought and memory left !

Peace, fond mourner ! This thy boon, —
Thou thyself must follow soon.

Peace, —and let repining go !
Peace, — for Fate will have it so.

Vainly now his praise is said :
Vain the garland for his head :

Yet is comfort's shadow cast
From the kindness of the past.

All my love could do to cheer
Warmed his heart when he was here.

Honour's plaudit, Friendship's vow
Did not coldly wait till now.

Oh, my comrade, oh, my friend,
If this parting be the end,

Yet I hold my life divine,
To have known a soul like thine:

And I hush the low lament
In submission, penitent.

Still the sun is in the skies :
He sets — but I have seen him rise !

PERDITA.

I WATCHED your ship where, strong and
      bright,
She sailed into the gathering night
      And sped away ;
I saw the sunset colours die
And gray gloom wrap the evening sky
      And veil the day.

I heard the cold waves on the shore
Their pensive sorrow o'er and o'er
      In murmurs tell,

While, as the glimmering sea grew dim,
The wind sang low its vesper hymn —
    Farewell, Farewell.

What thoughts of blessing and of prayer
I wafted on the twilight air,
    What fancies drear
Possessed my soul, no words could say —
Yet holy angels listening may
    Its homage hear.

I mused upon your parting word,
The low, sad whisper, scarcely heard,
    Your angel face,
And — fadeless flowers in memory's track —
The happy days, that come not back,
    Of fortune's grace :

Days when we roved on Avon's side,
Or wandered by the rushing tide
    Of bickering Stour,
Or in the great cathedral strayed —
Where to be worthy still I prayed
    Of one so pure.

The sunset mist, the golden town,
When we strolled home from Harbledown,
    The merry bands

Of rustic girls who bore, for sign
Of prospered toil, the fragrant vine
    In tawny hands;

The quiet streets, as evening fell,
The minster's gloom, the solemn bell,
    The scented air,
The rooks that thronged the giant trees,
The churchyard stones and, over these,
    The moonlight fair, —

I felt them all, as though that they
Had been the things of yesterday,
    And chill regret
Preyed on my lonely heart, to think
How soon the stars of pleasure sink
    And we forget.

The Thames is flowing, broad and free,
'Neath that old bridge of Battersea,
    Where, veiled in gloom,
Great St. John sleeps — too sound to wake,
For all the vows that lovers make
    Beside his tomb.

The emerald throstle's silver call
Is heard by Leicester's haunted hall,
    And down the vale

R

Of Kenilworth the hawthorns wreath,
And roses tremble, underneath
  The starlight pale.

The winds of night sigh softly through
The needles of St. Martin's yew,
  And round the shrines
Of gray St. Nicholas, the lone
And melancholy breezes moan,
  And ivy twines.

From those proud cliffs that smile on France
You still might see the moonbeams dance
  O'er midnight waves ; —
Are all the reveries sublime
And holy thoughts of that sweet time
  Lost in their graves ?

Is the light faded, has the ray
Of heaven become the common day,
  And from your breast
The careless warder Time let slip
The sense of fond companionship
  That was its guest ?

I will not think it — though, for me,
By day or night, by land or sea,
  Ah, nevermore

Can those exalted moments seem
Like aught but some bewildered dream
    Of fairy lore !

I do not think it — those clear eyes
The light that burns in paradise
    Is shining through ;
And all that radiant woman brought
Of holy faith and heavenly thought
    Is shrined in you !

Farewell, farewell — the sands of gold
Have run their course, the tale is told,
    And dark and fast
Night closes round my wandering way —
As round the set of that sad day
    Which was our last.

Yet ever, while we walk this earth,
In shade or shine, in grief or mirth,
    While life endures,
One thought must still our hearts entwine, —
And naught can take your place in mine,
    Nor mine in yours.

ARTHUR.

[1872-1886.]

I.

White sail upon the ocean verge,
  Just crimsoned by the setting sun,
Thou hast thy port beyond the surge,
  Thy happy homeward course to run,
And wingéd hope, with heart of fire,
To gain the bliss of thy desire.

I watch thee till the sombre sky
  Has darkly veiled the lucent plain;
My thoughts, like homeless spirits, fly
  Behind thee o'er the glimmering main:
Thy prow will kiss a golden strand,
But they can never come to land.

And if they could, the fanes are black
  Where once I bent the reverent knee;
No shrine would send an answer back,
  No sacred altar blaze for me,
No holy bell, with silver toll,
Declare the ransom of my soul.

'Tis equal darkness, here or there ;
   For nothing that this world can give
Could now the ravaged past repair,
   Or win the precious dead to live !
Life's crumbling ashes quench its flame,
And every place is now the same.

II.

Thou idol of my constant heart,
   Thou child of perfect love and light,
That sudden from my side didst part,
   And vanish in the sea of night,
Through whatsoever tempests blow
My weary soul with thine would go.

Say, if thy spirit yet have speech,
   What port lies hid within the pall,
What shore death's gloomy billows reach,
   Or if they reach no shore at all !
One word — one little word — to tell
That thou art safe and all is well !

The anchors of my earthly fate,
   As they were cast so must they cling ;
And naught is now to do but wait
   The sweet release that time will bring,
When all these mortal moorings break,
For one last voyage I must make.

Say that across the shuddering dark —
    And whisper that the hour is near —
Thy hand will guide my shattered bark
    Till mercy's radiant coasts appear,
Where I shall clasp thee to my breast,
And know once more the name of rest.

NOTES.

NOTES.

1. "The Broken Harp" — which was written in the vale of the Dargle — and "Asleep" have been set to melodies that are tender and lovely, by my friend Richard Mansfield.

2. My poem of "Orgia" has had a singular experience, the authorship of it having, periodically, been ascribed to various drunkards, lunatics, suicides, and other such eccentric persons, in whose pockets, after their death, have been found manuscript copies of it, in a chronic state of mangled metre and bad grammar. I wrote the poem on December 10, 1859, in Boston, and it was first published on January 7, 1860, in a paper called the *New York Saturday Press*, — long ago extinct.

3. "Love and Death" was delivered by me at the dedication of the Actors' Monument to Edgar Poe, in the Metropolitan Museum, New York, May 4, 1885. The poem was not written for that occasion, or for any occasion, but it was written just before that time, and I thought it appropriate to the commemoration of that poet.

4. This title, "The Voice of the Silence," originated and first used by me in 1876, was taken, many years later, and used in the same sense, by an eccentric writer on theosophy, the late Mme. Blavatsky.

5. At Boston, October 28, 1882, was commemorated the fiftieth anniversary of William Warren's

adoption of the profession of the stage. At midnight, after the play, at a supper in the comedian's home, No. 2 Bulfinch Place, a loving cup was presented to him, — the gift of Edwin Booth, Joseph Jefferson, Miss Mary Anderson, John McCullough, and Lawrence Barrett, — and, in offering that token, I read this poem.

6. The "Elegy at Evergreen" was first denominated "Anubis," the name of the Egyptian god who presided over the transit of souls across the river of death. The Actors' Monument is inscribed with two lines from Shakespeare: —

"The benediction of these covering heavens
Fall on their heads like dew."

And it also bears these inscriptions, written by me: —
In loving and reverent memory of many votaries of the stage, whose ashes are buried near it, this monument was placed here by the Actors' Fund of America, June, 1887.

Here to your eyes, our earthly labours done,
We who played many parts now play but one.
We knew the stops, could give the viol breath,
But now are only monitors of death:
Yet even thus our relics may impart
A truth beyond the reach of living art,
Teaching the strong, the beautiful, the brave,
That all life's pathways centre in the grave;
Bidding them live, nor negligent nor fond,
To bless this world, yet ever look beyond.

7. John T. Raymond is buried at Evergreen Cemetery, and his grave is marked with a stone bearing my lines, preceded by the following inscription: This monument, the gift of many affectionate

friends, is placed here in loving memory of John T.
Raymond, comedian. He was born in Buffalo, New
York, April 5, 1836. He died in Evansville, Indiana,
April 10, 1887.

> *'Hinc apicem rapax*
> *Fortuna cum stridore acuto*
> *Sustulit, hic posuisse gaudet.'*

8. Lester Wallack, the most brilliant and long the
most distinguished actor of high comedy on the
American stage, died on September 6, 1888. — Other
friends, named in these pages, have passed away.
John Brougham died on June 7, 1880; John Mc-
Cullough on November 8, 1885; William Warren on
September 21, 1888; John Gilbert on June 17, 1889;
George Fawcett Rowe on August 30, 1889; Lawrence Barrett on March 20, 1891; and Clifton W.
Tayleure on April 12, 1891. — Allusion occurs, in
the tribute to Lawrence Barrett, to Adelaide Neil-
son, who died on August 15, 1880, and to Edward
A. Sothern, who died on January 20, 1881. — The
poem called "Good Night" commemorates the
genial humourist of *Harper's Magazine,* William A.
Seaver. — William James Florence, whose epitaph
appears among my commemorative poems, is buried
at Greenwood. He was born in Albany, New York,
July 26, 1831, and he died in Philadelphia, November
19, 1891. — The tributes to Brougham, John Lawrence
Toole, George Fawcett Rowe, John Gilbert, Lawrence Barrett, and Lester Wallack were originally
delivered at festivals in their honour, at the Lotos
Club, New York. The feast to John Gilbert was
given to celebrate the completion of his fiftieth year
as an actor, November 30, 1878. The present writer
made an address, closing it with the poem here

given, which was originally called "Edelweiss."— The tributes to Edwin Booth, John McCullough, and Henry Irving were delivered, on festival occasions, at Delmonico's. "Honour's Pearl" was also delivered there. "Thure et Fidibus" was read at the Lotos Club. The former was a poem of farewell to the Hon. Whitelaw Reid, just before he went abroad as American Minister to France; the latter a poem of welcome to him when he came home.

Most of my poems have drifted into life: they came; they were not compelled; and therefore, and because their existence seems frail and their fate dubious, I have called them WANDERERS. They are the vagrant children of my love, and perhaps partiality has blinded judgment and persuaded me to anticipate for them a permanence to which they are not destined. I have thought that they express representative moods of feeling and representative phases of experience, and that their style is distinctive. The wish to add something of permanent value to pure literature is honourable and not unnatural; and I am willing to believe that these poems, thoughtfully chosen out of many that I have written, are an authentic contribution to that ancient body of English lyrical poetry of which gentleness is the soul and simplicity the garment. If this estimate of them is wrong, oblivion will soon set it right.

W. W.

July 15, 1892.